Loving Jesus, Loving Like Jesus

A 40-day Lenten Devotional

LOVING JESUS,
LOVING LIKE JESUS

Executive Director, CC Global
MAXIE DUNNAM

CC Global Coordinator
MIKE WEAVER

Book Design by
THAXTON STUDIOS

Christ Church Communications Director
JO ELLEN DRUELINGER

NOTE: The engravings featured in this book are the work of
Gustave Doré (January 6, 1832-January 23, 1883). Doré was born in
France and lived the last part of his life in London. He is probably most
famous for his depictions of numerous scenes from the Bible. The scans
used here were made available by Felix Just, S.J. Visit his site to see more.
(http://catholic-resources.org/Art/Dore.htm)

LOVING JESUS, LOVING LIKE JESUS

A 40-DAY LENTEN DEVOTIONAL

by

SHANE STANFORD

AND MEMBERS OF

CHRIST UNITED METHODIST CHURCH

MEMPHIS, TENNESSEE

COMPILED BY TOM FUERST

EDITED BY SARAH PHELAN & ANTHONY THAXTON

Introduction

Cassie Fuerst

Welcome friends to **Lent**.

Welcome to a season of **reflection**...

- Reflecting on Jesus' suffering and humility

- Reflecting on Christ's image in us

- Reflecting on our own spiritual health

Welcome to a season of **repentance**...

- Repenting from sins breaking our fellowship with Christ

- Repenting from idols

- Repenting from our self-centeredness

Welcome to a season of **fasting**...

- Fasting from things taking our attention from our Savior

- Fasting from our luxuries so others can have necessities

- Fasting from our obsessions and addictions

Welcome friend. Welcome to the season of Lent.

Think of Lent as your yearly spiritual checkup: a time to take a thorough look at where you are heading, what controls you, how you spend your time, who surrounds you and why you do the things you do.

Repentance

Any journey to spiritual vitality must begin with repentance. Unconfessed sin not only damages our relationship with God, but it also damages our relationships with all those around us. Confession cleanses the soul. Repentance turns us back to the narrow path.

Fasting

For many of us to get in spiritual shape, fasting is a necessity. Fasting means intentionally abstaining from an object or an activity with the end goal of replacing the thing with concentrated focus on God or God's people. As you reflect, you might notice media distracts you from life. If this is so, maybe you need to fast from TV or Facebook. Or you might discover you consume more food than your fair share. You might decide to fast from a certain meal or a particular food. Fasting is hard. At the beginning, you are more focused on the discomfort, *but hold on to the end.* God will reveal Himself through this discipline. Remember, Sundays are not fast days but feast days. Think of them as mini Easters until we celebrate our Savior's resurrection fully in April.

Laying Down and Taking Up

Finally, Lent is not only of a season of laying down but also of taking up. What has God been leading you to do but you have been putting off? Do you need to join a small group? What about taking walks with your Savior? How about committing 15 minutes a day to abandoned play with your kids? Is there someone who needs your compassion?

Welcome friend. Welcome to the season of Lent. May we be forever changed as we walk with the Savior to the cross!

HOW TO USE THIS BOOK

Each week of Lent will have five days of devotional material running Monday through Friday. Then you will also see a devotional on Sunday from pastor Shane Stanford. Each day will have a prayer, a scripture reading, a devotional thought and a series of reflection questions with space provided to write answers.

You will gain the most from this book if you do it with a group of people. It is designed so that you can do it individually and then come together in your small group or Sunday school class to reflect on the devotions and questions together.

Loving Jesus, Loving Like Jesus

Foreword by
Shane Stanford

Scripture teaches us that what we believe about God matters. In Deuteronomy, we are warned to be careful to follow God's commandments. These ten commandments fall into two primary categories: 1) To Love God, and 2) To Love God's People.

Jesus echoes this teaching when asked by a certain religious leader, "What is the greatest commandment?" Jesus answers that the "greatest commandment is to love the Lord your God with all your heart, soul and mind." But, he then continues, "The second commandment is as important as the first—to love your neighbor as yourself."

Therefore, we believe that the entire message of the Good News is summarized in these two commandments. Our translation of these commandments as related to our Mission as a congregation at Christ Church is to "Love Jesus and Love Like Jesus." Therefore, we believe this commitment is more than a nice slogan, but embodies the very heart of who we are called to be as the Body of Christ.

Loving Jesus

Loving Jesus is more than just our faith in him. In fact, Jesus himself states that even the "evildoers believe in God." No, to "love Jesus" requires spending time with him and building a relationship with him. We must commit ourselves to knowing the person, purpose and plan of Jesus' life and teachings. The Biblical model for loving Jesus is experienced best in three ways:

A. Study and Devotion: We believe that every person must spend time in God's Word. Although we believe that daily devotions are essential, they are not enough. The deeper we explore the life and teachings of Jesus, the more we know the person of Christ. This relationship is the foundation of our faith.

B. Prayer: We believe that every person must spend time communicating with God. Prayer is a two-way street. Though sharing our concerns and requests are part of our prayer life, we must also spend time being in God's presence and hearing from God. The Lord's Prayer is a primary tool for organizing a person's prayer life. Jesus mentioned several areas of the Lord's Prayer that help each of us develop a deeper prayer experience.

1. Praise and Adoration
2. Seeking God's Will
3. Request for Our Earthly Needs and Concerns
4. Guidance and a Clear Path Away from the Temptations of the World
5. Protection from the Adversary

C. Spiritual Disciplines: We believe every person opens their heart and life to God by practicing the spiritual disciplines of fasting, serving, tithing and intercession. The Disciplines provide a deeper connection to Christ and expand our prayer and devotional lives by offering a context for how we see Christ work in our daily journey.

Loving Like Jesus

"Loving Like Jesus" is more than doing good works or following the example of Christ. We believe that every person has been gifted to share Christ in the world in a unique way. The spiritual gifts of God's people provide various means for serving as the Body of Christ in the world.

The Biblical Model for "Loving Like Jesus" is expressed in four ways:

A. Seeking the Lost: Jesus actively sought those far from God. In one encounter after another, Jesus offered opportunities for people to not only find God, but to start a new life. The Church must be a place where those far from God can find rest for their journey and then begin again.

B. Caring for the Broken: Jesus cared for the sick and broken by loving them, accepting them and healing their wounds. The Church must be a place where the sick and broken find healing, rest and hope. As Jesus stated, "A doctor does not come to the well but to the sick." The Church must first be a hospital for the sick and broken.

C. Standing up for Justice: Much of Jesus' earthly ministry was spent advocating for justice. Jesus met the marginalized and those living at the city gates not only in their place but in the depth of their suffering and sorrow. The Church must be a place where those who have been forgotten by the world find a new home of righteousness and justice.

D. Serving the Least of These: Jesus met and served the "least of these" as part of his daily life. In Matthew 25, he teaches that the Church meets HIS needs when we take time to meet the needs of those who are the "least of these our brothers and sisters." The Church must be a place where those without the basic needs and opportunities of life can find an identity and support as part of the family of God.

So, remember, the following devotional guide is an opportunity to:

      1) learn more about knowing and following Christ
      2) live more faithfully as the hands and feet of Jesus in the world
      3) love deeply the way that Christ has loved us
      4) look after those for whom Christ has said the world has forgotten

Our prayer during this next study season is that you not only learn more about Christ, but that you invite Christ to be the Lord of your life and the Leader of your journey from here. Nothing we *know* can substitute for first *being known* by God.

Holy God, we come before You as withered trees: dry, dying and unable to bear fruit. Our seeds are shriveled and fall on hard soil. Our leaves are scorched by the sun of Your righteous judgment. Take Your pruning shears, O Lord, cut away our dead branches and throw them in the fire. But please, Lord, do not chop us down. Spare us the axe. Instead, we ask that You would dig us up and plant us again beside streams of living water. Bring us back to health through Your Son Jesus, the source of all life. Let us bear fruit in and out of season. May our lives feed others and give shade to the weary. Amen.

Joel 1:1-2, 12-17 (NIV)

¹The word of the Lord that came to Joel son of Pethuel.
²Hear this, you elders;
   listen, all who live in the land.
Has anything like this ever happened in your days
   or in the days of your ancestors?

***

¹²The vine is dried up
   and the fig tree is withered;
the pomegranate, the palm and the apple tree—
   all the trees of the field—are dried up.
Surely the people's joy
   is withered away.
¹³Put on sackcloth, you priests, and mourn;
   wail, you who minister before the altar.
Come, spend the night in sackcloth,
   you who minister before my God;
for the grain offerings and drink offerings
   are withheld from the house of your God.
¹⁴Declare a holy fast;
   call a sacred assembly.
Summon the elders
   and all who live in the land
to the house of the Lord your God,
   and cry out to the Lord.
¹⁵Alas for that day!
   For the day of the Lord is near;
   it will come like destruction from the Almighty.
¹⁶Has not the food been cut off
   before our very eyes—
joy and gladness

from the house of our God?
¹⁷The seeds are shriveled
  beneath the clods.
The storehouses are in ruins,
  the granaries have been broken down,
    for the grain has dried up.

Devotion

Here's a quick Lenten quiz:

> •Lent lasts for 40 days and runs from Ash Wednesday to Easter. *True or False?*
>
> •Lent is about self-denial. *True or False?*
>
> •There are more than 40 days between Ash Wednesday and Easter. *True or False?*
>
> •Lenten fasting does not include Sundays, which are always feast days. *True or False?*
>
> •Lent is about repentance. *True or False?*

The answer to all of the above questions is true, but I find, in the church circles I run in, that we normally get only the first two questions right. (If you got all five, a gold star for you.)

Being raised in a fairly typical Protestant household, I would have scored a solid 'F' on the above quiz. Still, we *practiced* Lent at our house even if we didn't fully understand it. My mother, sister and I all gave up something. Normally this was something dessert related. We understood that Lent was supposed to be a time of deprivation; though the adjoining fact that this was also supposed to help us develop *discipline* was rarely discussed. We picked an easy thing like chocolate to sacrifice for 46 days. (Again, as a child I had never heard that Lent didn't include Sundays.) But the equally important truth about Lent, that it's a time of *repentance*, never came on the radar.

When we turn to the Old Testament, however, we see that fasting seasons were not, first and foremost, about *self-denial to help develop discipline*. Folks fasted out of sorrow for their *sin*.

We see this very clearly in the passage from Joel. Joel, the prophet, speaks to Judah after God has sent a terrible plague of locusts to destroy their crops. The locusts have eaten everything, leaving the people desperate for food. Their joy is "withered up." In response, Joel does not call them to "cheer up" but instead to "mourn" before the Lord, to fast and to prepare themselves for the day of the Lord.

Faithful Jews were called to *repent* for the sin that brought God's punishment, and also called to prepare for the coming presence of God through the outpouring of his Spirit.

Joel 2:28, 30-32a says,

> "And afterward, I will pour out my Spirit on all people. Your sons and daughters will prophesy, your old men will dream dreams, your young men will see visions. I will show wonders in the heavens and on the earth, blood and fire and billows of smoke. The sun will be turned to darkness and the moon to blood before the coming of the great and dreadful day of the Lord. And everyone who calls on the name of the Lord will be saved."

The crazy thing for us now is that the Day of the Lord has come! Jesus has made it so that everyone who calls on His name *will* be saved. His Spirit *is* being poured out on all kinds of people. And yet we still turn away from God's salvation.

This Easter we will celebrate the resurrection of Jesus, so let us prepare our hearts by repenting of our sin. The good news, again, comes from the prophet Joel. "'Even now,' declares the Lord, 'return to me with all your heart, with fasting and weeping and mourning.' Rend your heart and not your garments. Return to the Lord your God, for he is gracious and compassionate, slow to anger and abounding in love…" (2:12-13)

Reflection Questions

•How are you preparing your heart for Easter?

_____

_____

•If you were face-to-face with Jesus right now, would you rejoice or mourn?

_____

_____

_____

•What is God calling you to repent of in this season?

_____

_____

_____

•Take some time for self-reflection. Imagine you were face-to-face with Jesus. What would He ask you to repent of? How would He ask you to prepare yourself so that you can rejoice in His presence?

My harsh judging of others. My synical bitter heart. He might ask that I pray more form deliverance from this place, be less self-absorbed. Read the Bible for instruction.

God, sometimes I just don't want to face You. I know the ways I have failed You. I feel like a disappointment to You. So as much as I would like to hide from You, I know You are all-knowing and see my shortcomings. Please show me the curtains I try to hide behind, and help me to tear them down and to come to You in a spirit of repentance. Have mercy on me, O God, according to Your unfailing love. And create in me a clean heart, and renew a right spirit within me. Amen.

Psalm 51 (ESV)

¹Have mercy on me, O God,
    according to your steadfast love;
according to your abundant mercy
    blot out my transgressions.
²Wash me thoroughly from my iniquity,
    and cleanse me from my sin!

³For I know my transgressions,
    and my sin is ever before me.
⁴Against you, you only, have I sinned
    and done what is evil in your sight,
so that you may be justified in your words
    and blameless in your judgment.
⁵Behold, I was brought forth in iniquity,
    and in sin did my mother conceive me.
⁶Behold, you delight in truth in the inward being,
    and you teach me wisdom in the secret heart.

⁷Purge me with hyssop, and I shall be clean;
    wash me, and I shall be whiter than snow.
⁸Let me hear joy and gladness;
    let the bones that you have broken rejoice.
⁹Hide your face from my sins,
    and blot out all my iniquities.
¹⁰Create in me a clean heart, O God,
    and renew a right spirit within me.
¹¹Cast me not away from your presence,
    and take not your Holy Spirit from me.
¹²Restore to me the joy of your salvation,
    and uphold me with a willing spirit.

¹³Then I will teach transgressors your ways,
    and sinners will return to you.
¹⁴Deliver me from bloodguiltiness, O God,
    O God of my salvation,

and my tongue will sing aloud of your righteousness.
¹⁵O Lord, open my lips,
    and my mouth will declare your praise.
¹⁶For you will not delight in sacrifice, or I would give it;
    you will not be pleased with a burnt offering.
¹⁷The sacrifices of God are a broken spirit;
    a broken and contrite heart, O God, you will not despise.

¹⁸Do good to Zion in your good pleasure;
    build up the walls of Jerusalem;
¹⁹then will you delight in right sacrifices,
    in burnt offerings and whole burnt offerings;
    then bulls will be offered on your altar.

Devotion

A fond memory of my childhood is watching *The Wizard of Oz* every year. Maybe it wasn't on TV every year, but it sure seemed like it. And one of the most memorable scenes is when that curious dog Toto pulls back the curtain to reveal the 'great and powerful Oz' to be neither very great nor to have all that much power. He's just an ordinary guy with some secrets to hide—like not being great and powerful.

Do you ever feel like just hiding behind a curtain? You know the things you have done, the people you have hurt, the ways you have sinned against God and your fellow man, and you think, "Man, I hope no one finds out." So you slink behind the curtain and perhaps peek out just long enough to make sure nobody saw you go back there.

David felt that way. He knew that his sin with Bathsheba did not exactly coincide with being a 'man after God's own heart.' So he did everything within his power to hide behind that curtain, which included cover-ups, lies and murder. Thinking he had gotten away with it all, he had no idea the prophet Nathan knew about anything, when in reality, he was pulling back David's curtain to reveal the sad truth of David's life. David may have been able to pull the wool over everyone else's eyes, but God sees all and revealed David's sin to Nathan.

Psalm 51 is David's reaction to being found out.

He is a broken man. His curtain has been ripped from its rod, and he is laid bare before a holy God. He can no longer hide. His only recourse is to fall on his face in humble repentance and to cry out for mercy and reconciliation. And now he desires a clean heart and a right spirit—a heart that longs for the heart of God, and a spirit that no longer opts for hiding behind the curtain.

Here's the thing: there is no curtain with God. As much as we would like to hide, scripture reminds us that our sins will find us out. Translation: He already knows. So why bother trying to hide? Doesn't it make more sense, instead of waiting until someone calls us on the carpet, to just go ahead and cry out to the one who loves us and truly wants what's best for us? He is great, and He is powerful. But He is also love. Cry out to Him.

Reflection Questions

•What are you trying to hide behind the curtain? From whom are you trying to hide?

_____

_____

_____

_____

•What keeps you from being real?

_____

_____

_____

_____

•What will it take for you to fall on your face before God in humble repentance?

_____

_____

_____

_____

Lord, today may we be reconnected, reclaimed and reconciled back to You, the one who does not change. Amen.

2 Corinthians 5:20b-6:10 (RSV)

[20]So we are ambassadors for Christ, God making his appeal through us. We beseech you on behalf of Christ, be reconciled to God. [21]For our sake he made him to be sin who knew no sin, so that in him we might become the righteousness of God.

[1]Working together with him, then, we entreat you not to accept the grace of God in vain. [2]For he says,

> "At the acceptable time I have listened to you,
> and helped you on the day of salvation."

Behold, now is the acceptable time; behold, now is the day of salvation. [3]We put no obstacle in any one's way, so that no fault may be found with our ministry, [4]but as servants of God we commend ourselves in every way: through great endurance, in afflictions, hardships, calamities, [5]beatings, imprisonments, tumults, labors, watching, hunger; [6]by purity, knowledge, forbearance, kindness, the Holy Spirit, genuine love, [7]truthful speech, and the power of God; with the weapons of righteousness for the right hand and for the left; [8]in honor and dishonor, in ill repute and good repute. We are treated as impostors, and yet are true; [9]as unknown, and yet well known; as dying, and behold we live; as punished, and yet not killed; [10]as sorrowful, yet always rejoicing; as poor, yet making many rich; as having nothing, and yet possessing everything.

Devotion

This is a fascinating passage. Take in mind that the Corinthian letters were written to a very impressionable church. Corinth was a trade city at an important cross-road in the Roman Empire. The church was likely made up of mostly freed slaves who found work in the ports and trade centers. They were a group of people who were still learning how to live for themselves. The Corinthian church had many different philosophies trying to influence it.

Knowing this, Paul uses a rhetorical tool that would be familiar to them. Philosophers and sages of this time would list their struggles and virtues to build up credibility above others. Often, they would present apparent opposites to use their opponent's arguments against them. Whoever had the most popular philosophy during the debate was deemed the "winner."

Instead of being concerned with what was popular, Paul implored them to look toward the salvation of Jesus, the one who suffered virtuously on their behalf. Jesus' message is so important, Paul himself models His life. This salvation doesn't change like the popular philosophies of the moment or circumstances. If fact, possessing this salvation meant possessing everything.

Lent is a time for our lives to be brought back into focus, remembering our salvation and letting go of all that is temporary. In doing so, we will be reconnected, reclaimed and reconciled back to God, which is everything.

Reflection Questions

•How often have I let myself get swept up in popular opinion, forgetting what is true?

_____

_____

_____

•Or been "tossed about" by circumstances, losing sight of what is important, and in doing so received "grace in vain"?

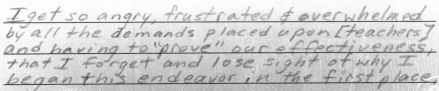

I get so angry, frustrated & overwhelmed by all the demands placed upon [teachers] and having to "prove" our effectiveness, that I forget and lose sight of why I began this endeavor in the first place.

Sunday

SHANE STANFORD

JOHN 19

A friend of mine recently traveled to Kenya to visit a day orphanage for children who have lost parents to the HIV/AIDS crisis. In Kenya, as in other nations in sub-Saharan Africa, the needs created by the pandemic have overrun the institutional services, especially those that serve children. Day orphanages exist as a means of providing basic necessities to those little ones who would otherwise have nothing—truly a last resort for these, the "least of these" among us.

Arriving at the orphanage, my friend met two workers carrying a small girl. Her body was frail and clearly malnourished, but her face wore the most beautiful smile. Whereas her body revealed every sign of what is most disturbing and troubling about the plight of those in her situation, her face revealed a spirit that was anything but hopeless.

As these contrasting images collided in my friend's mind, she greeted the young child with the help of an interpreter. My friend learned that the child's father had died just after she was born; her mother died when she was 3. She lived with an aunt who was also sick and who could not provide much in the way of care. In fact, the child told my friend that it was *she who* cared for her aunt at night, trying to provide her with as much comfort as possible. Like so many in similar circumstances, this child lived a hard, lonely existence.

Every morning, the workers arrived in a "goat cart" and took the child to the day orphanage. Here she found not only food and an occasional change of clothes, but also friends and others with whom she could talk and play. Sure, the toys were few, the meals meager and the clothes secondhand, but this place in the daylight seemed worlds away from her home at night, and it provided small, if fleeting, glimpses of hope.

My friend listened intently as the workers and the little girl described her daily routine. "We pick her up," they said in their broken English, "and bring her here so that she might find a little food, some clothes and some schooling. It is not much, but it is more than she has when she returns to *Miseri.*"

"Where?" my friend asked, not sure that she had heard right.

"*Miseri,*" the worker replied. "It is the name of her settlement. The word comes from the Swahili for 'Egypt.'"

My friend realized that although she had not heard our English word "misery," it certainly conveyed the right meaning. "Misery" was more than appropriate to describe the child's life. After all, what hope did she have? She most likely would not grow up to finish school, train for a job, have a family, or for that matter, enjoy an abundant childhood like the kids my friend knew in the States. No, the chances of her having a future were those same impossible odds the disease of hopelessness brings to everyone who suffers from it—but, for my friend, these obstacles were all the more tragic because now they had a face.

Standing there, my friend was lost in thought, musing over how impossible it all seemed for this little girl. *Where was God? Where was hope? What could effectively confront the wake of her struggle, not only for this child but for all children? What could possibly fill the void left by such desolation of this child's future?* She paused a moment, lost in the realization of such sorrow. But then, as she looked up, she again saw the child's smile and the embrace of the workers, their love and care for this little one. Above all, she saw that in spite of the obvious struggles, this picture seemed full of possibilities, not because the circumstances she faced weren't daunting, but because there was something hopeful about the scene. Surrounded by so much sorrow and despair, my friend saw something amazing— an answer to her questions.

Her answer was right in front of her, resting in what she had almost missed. My friend realized that despite the disease of pandemic poverty and the impossible circumstances for this child, nothing was set in stone. No. Why? Because these people who loved like Jesus, touched like Jesus, cared like Jesus—who had become Jesus to this child—ensured that *misery* was not all she would know.

A friend once told me that God is not afraid of our doubts, our questions or our anger. What God does not like is when we turn away and think we can do this on our own. And His sadness deepens when we believe that our journey is just somehow too screwed up to have any redemptive meaning.

Think about the life and death of Jesus: Have you ever wondered why Jesus was born, lived a normal life, launched a ministry and *then* provided for the salvation of the world? God work through His Son, Jesus, didn't just rectify some cosmic, spiritual debt. No, God knew the power of what His redemption and chance for a new life would mean— and so the God of the Universe became like us. God took on a story Himself, showed us through *everything* there is a reason for which to survive, hope and learn.

Before Jesus, the people of God understood their relationship with God from only one angle: God was up there (in the sky, in the fire, on a mountain, in the Temple) and they were down here. All that happened at Calvary changed that. The story got personal for God—and for you and me.

Take a look at Jesus' last words on the cross:

> *Father, forgive them* . . . (Luke 23:34)
> *Why have you forsaken Me?* . . . (Matthew 27:46)
> *Take care of My mother* . . . (John 19:26-27)
> *I am thirsty* . . . (John 19:28)
> *I am through with this* . . . (John 19:30)

Do those prayers sound familiar to you? They do to me. Why? Because in one form or another, I have prayed them, too. Haven't you? Reading those words reminds me that Jesus knows what it is like to hurt, to care about others, to be frustrated, to feel forgotten and to be exhausted. And, if Jesus knows all of these things, then He must also know what it is like to wonder if the whole journey is worth it (*Oh, that's right, the Garden of Gethsemane*)-- what it is like to lose a loved one (*Yes, I remember Jesus cried for Lazarus*)-- what it is like to feel betrayed and forgotten (*Did you just think about Judas?*).

Because He became like us, Jesus knows what it's like to be in our shoes.

> --To hurt, both on the inside and outside
> --To lose people you love
> --To keep saying the same thing and feel as if no one is listening
> --To give away with little hope of receiving anything in return

God also knows that things are not lost, just unfound…that tough situations have deeper meanings…that creation comes from chaos and that hope comes from struggle.

God knows that one step does not the whole journey make.

However, the most important thing … the unforgettable thing … the most incredible thing: God knows *you* and God knows *me*, and that is our new beginning and our hope.

I am not sure where or when you are reading this book, but I'm glad you are. Sit back, relax and plan to stay awhile. God has something amazing in store for you, not because of any words that I could write, but because God desperately wants you to see that no life is beyond restoring, no misery so great that it does not hold within it the possibility of redemption.

Reflection Questions

Many of us have felt the same hopelessness and fear as the story above. *Can God forgive my past? Will Christ accept my meager pleas? Is it possible for God to love me even when I doubt or feel unsure? Does God even care?*

Whether you believe it or not in this moment, we serve a God who loves us passionately and who is neither afraid of our mistakes nor repelled by our fears.

Consider for a moment the potential of God's love for you and of a life restored.

•What are the broken places in your life that keep you living in misery? Make a list of your broken places, whether dreams, mistakes or relationships.

Trying to make my mother's life more pleasant for her. Trying to make her happy, yet make sure she is safe

•What keeps those broken places from being restored?

Her disease will not let her find happiness, in any circumstance.

•What "first steps" do you need to undertake in order to heal?

Figure out how to detach from her uncontrollabe unhappiness; learn to compartmentalize it.

•Why is it important for the Church to live life together as a means for helping one another heal the broken places of our lives?

To encourage one another, and watch out for one another when & if we go astray. To remind one another that no situation is too hopeless that God's love for us would not endure.

Dear Heavenly Father, help us draw closer to You. We want to live solely for You, but we tend to worry about appearances and what others will think rather than pleasing You by our actions and words. Let us bring our inner and outer lives together. Amen.

Matthew 6:1-6, 16-21 (NIV)

"¹Be careful not to practice your righteousness in front of others to be seen by them. If you do, you will have no reward from your Father in heaven.

²"So when you give to the needy, do not announce it with trumpets, as the hypocrites do in the synagogues and on the streets, to be honored by others. Truly I tell you, they have received their reward in full. ³But when you give to the needy, do not let your left hand know what your right hand is doing, ⁴so that your giving may be in secret. Then your Father, who sees what is done in secret, will reward you.

⁵"And when you pray, do not be like the hypocrites, for they love to pray standing in the synagogues and on the street corners to be seen by others. Truly I tell you, they have received their reward in full. ⁶But when you pray, go into your room, close the door and pray to your Father, who is unseen. Then your Father, who sees what is done in secret, will reward you.

***

¹⁶"When you fast, do not look somber as the hypocrites do, for they disfigure their faces to show others they are fasting. Truly I tell you, they have received their reward in full. ¹⁷But when you fast, put oil on your head and wash your face, ¹⁸so that it will not be obvious to others that you are fasting, but only to your Father, who is unseen; and your Father, who sees what is done in secret, will reward you.

¹⁹"Do not store up for yourselves treasures on earth, where moths and vermin destroy, and where thieves break in and steal. ²⁰But store up for yourselves treasures in heaven, where moths and vermin do not destroy, and where thieves do not break in and steal. ²¹For where your treasure is, there your heart will be also."

Devotion

Almost all of us live two lives—what people see on the outside, skin out, and what is really going on on the inside, skin in.

As a child, we learn what actions will bring pleasure to our parents, grandparents and friends. In school, we learn what outward signs of attention will please the teacher. On a sports court, we learn what skills will impress a coach. At the job, we learn to "put on a good front" whenever the boss is around. It is like wearing masks; we style our hair, select our clothes, join clubs, play sports and buy our houses and cars to impress those around us.

Matthew 6 announces that the time has come for us to change not just skin out, but also the skin in. In Jesus' day, people wore somber and hungry looks during a fast, they prayed grandiosely if people were watching and some even wore Bible verses strapped to their bodies to impress others with their biblical knowledge. We see that even today. Jesus blasts the hypocrisy behind such practices. God is not fooled by appearances. We cannot fake behavior to impress Him. He knows that inside the best of us lurk dark thoughts of pride, jealousy, lust and hatred. In His famous Sermon on the Mount, Jesus presents a radical way of life, free of pretense.

Matthew 6:1-4 is about giving to the needy in a way that only God will see. We all like to help and reach out, but some of us expect something in return, a big thank you, acknowledgment from others, even publicity. Jesus tells us, "So when you give to the needy, do not announce it with trumpets, as the hypocrites do in the synagogues and on the streets, to be honored by others…But when you give to the needy, do not let your left hand know what your right hand is doing, so that your giving may be in secret. Then your Father, who sees what is done in secret, will reward you."

Matthew 6:5 talks about prayer and praying unseen by others. Again, Jesus talks about the hypocrites who shout prayers loudly from the street corners, in church, and some who babble on like pagans—thinking they will be heard because of their many words. That does not impress God either! The Bible says that when you pray, go into a closet and communicate with God directly and personally. Again He will reward you! I am not suggesting you stop praying out loud and together, but pray to Him as your audience and not for others to be impressed by your words and your knowledge.

According to Matthew 6:16, fasting can be a life-changing experience, but despite this, it is one of the most neglected spiritual admonitions. It seems to be one of the most misunderstood and least practiced, and yet, through fasting and prayer, the Holy Spirit can transform lives. Some people show their fasting experience as they did in biblical times walking round in public with gaunt, somber faces to call attention to themselves. Some people participate in fasting weekends to be with friends like at a party and brag about it afterwards. When done for the wrong reasons to attract attention they are no different then the people in Jesus's time who fasted to impress each other with showy outward behavior.

Athletic Ministry has chosen Colossians 3:23 as our Bible verse, and I believe the verse ties into Matthew 6. Colossians 3:23: "Whatever you do, work at it with all your heart, as working for the Lord, not for men." Our shepherd coaches teach the children to give 100 percent, not for cheers and accolades, not to call attention to oneself, but to do it from the inside out, to please and glorify God.

Reflection Questions

•Do other people see what you are really like on the inside, or do they just know you for your outward appearance?

_____

_____

•Have you spent time trying to impress others with your generosity and service?

_____

_____

_____

_____

•What can you do today to change and grow closer to God and be the person He has called you to be?

_____

_____

_____

WEEK 2 | DAY 2 | TUESDAY
Genesis 2:15-17, 3:1-7 | Carolyn Culberson

Lord, we praise You for your faithfulness even in the face of our unfaithfulness. We praise You for the love You freely give us even though we have darkened our hearts with sin and death. Most of all, we praise You for Your victory on the cross and Your sovereign grace that allows us to cast our sins onto Your Son and claim His birthright as our own. Show us and convict us of that sin which weighs us down and prevents us from being able to walk with You in freedom and life. Amen.

Genesis 2:15-17, 3:1-7 (NIV)

¹⁵The Lord God took the man and put him in the Garden of Eden to work it and take care of it. ¹⁶And the Lord God commanded the man, "You are free to eat from any tree in the garden; ¹⁷but you must not eat from the tree of the knowledge of good and evil, for when you eat from it you will certainly die."

***

¹Now the serpent was more crafty than any of the wild animals the Lord God had made. He said to the woman, "Did God really say, 'You must not eat from any tree in the garden'?"

²The woman said to the serpent, "We may eat fruit from the trees in the garden, ³but God did say, 'You must not eat fruit from the tree that is in the middle of the garden, and you must not touch it, or you will die.'"

⁴"You will not certainly die," the serpent said to the woman. ⁵"For God knows that when you eat from it your eyes will be opened, and you will be like God, knowing good and evil."

⁶When the woman saw that the fruit of the tree was good for food and pleasing to the eye, and also desirable for gaining wisdom, she took some and ate it. She also gave some to her husband, who was with her, and he ate it. ⁷Then the eyes of both of them were opened, and they realized they were naked; so they sewed fig leaves together and made coverings for themselves.

Devotion

We cannot fully grasp the value of the Gospel until we understand the depth of our own sinfulness. This makes sense because a man cannot grasp that he has been saved until he understands that he was in danger.

The command God gave Adam in Genesis 2 is clear: "Do not eat from the tree or you will surely die." The consequence for sin is very clearly laid out: death. God doesn't tell us that when we disobey Him, His punishment will be a traffic jam on our way to work, or that we won't receive that promotion we've been working toward. The danger of an unrepentant heart before the Lord is a death so final and black that nothing but the direct intervention of God could save us.

We can see our own sinfulness reflected in that of Eve's when she takes the fruit in Genesis 3. Her heart is so easily swayed by the serpent into believing that God is holding out on her. She is convinced that there is something better for her than the blessings and plans God has already set before her. Eve believes this so strongly that she ignores the Lord's will for her life and reaches out to take her future into her own hands. We know what happens next: things go horribly wrong.

Unfortunately, many of us do not enjoy the thought of regularly meditating on our own sins and shortcomings. Why can't we just accept that God has provided salvation without our needing to give too close a look to that selfishness or greed or pride that has darkened our souls before Him?

Ironically, it is there in the midst of grief over our sins against the Father that we can find overwhelming joy and restoration in the blood of Jesus.

This Lenten season is a time for meditating on our sin. It may be uncomfortable or hard to do for any length of time because it is an act that is so contrary to what this world tells us is important. But it is through this meditation that we can truly discover the value and personal victory that Jesus achieves on the cross this Easter.

Reflection Questions

•What is the difference between our culture's attitude toward sin and God's attitude toward sin?

_____

_____

_____

_____

•To which attitude do we most regularly subscribe?

_____

•What sins do we have in our life that we need to repent to the Lord in order to move toward restoration?

_____

_____

_____

_____

_____

_____

Dear Heavenly Father, thank You for making forgiveness available to all of us. Please help us to continue to grow in Your love and understanding. We continue to pray for Your blessings on us, and we ask these things in Christ's name. Amen.

Psalm 32 (NIV)

[1]Blessed is the one
   whose transgressions are forgiven,
   whose sins are covered.
[2]Blessed is the one
   whose sin the Lord does not count against them
   and in whose spirit is no deceit.
[3]When I kept silent,
   my bones wasted away
   through my groaning all day long.
[4]For day and night
   your hand was heavy on me;
my strength was sapped
   as in the heat of summer.[b]
[5]Then I acknowledged my sin to you
   and did not cover up my iniquity.
I said, "I will confess
   my transgressions to the Lord."
And you forgave
   the guilt of my sin.
[6]Therefore let all the faithful pray to you
   while you may be found;
surely the rising of the mighty waters
   will not reach them.
[7]You are my hiding place;
   you will protect me from trouble
   and surround me with songs of deliverance.
[8]I will instruct you and teach you in the way you should go;
   I will counsel you with my loving eye on you.
[9]Do not be like the horse or the mule,
   which have no understanding
but must be controlled by bit and bridle
   or they will not come to you.
[10]Many are the woes of the wicked,
   but the Lord's unfailing love
   surrounds the one who trusts in him.
[11]Rejoice in the Lord and be glad, you righteous;
   sing, all you who are upright in heart!

Devotion

Psalm 32 is a psalm of hope and forgiveness. The hope is expressed in the first two verses where the psalmist, who is thought to be David, expresses that the Lord will not hold sin against us provided we take appropriate actions.

This concept was forward thinking when considering that the psalm was written approximately 850-900 years before Christ came and established that salvation and forgiveness were gifts based on faith instead of being attained through law and works.

Scholars think David wrote this psalm after he committed adultery with Bathsheba and the secret that he bore "sapped his strength." David had been weighted down with the guilt of the wrongful act, and it was not until he acknowledged his sin to the Lord and asked for forgiveness that he got relief.

The remainder of the psalm is joyful in that David received strength from the Lord and knew that the Lord provided him readily available shelter. This shelter is personified by the feelings that life without guilt brings to us.

David also asserts that if we trust the Lord, we will learn how to have a relationship with Him and develop an understanding that will keep us surrounded in God's love.

Our takeaway from this is that God will forgive us, but we must take action by acknowledging our sins to Him and removing any secrets we harbor. By doing so, our understanding of God coupled with peace and serenity will be enhanced and our lives will be more fulfilled.

Reflection Questions

•What feelings did David have that were the catalyst for writing this psalm?

_____

_____

•What are the side effects and other implications connected with having secrets of wrongdoing?

_____

_____

•Explain the reference to the horse and mule in verse 9 as it relates to the overall theme of this psalm.

_____

_____

Romans 5:12-19

¹²Therefore, just as sin entered the world through one man, and death through sin, and in this way death came to all people, because all sinned—

¹³To be sure, sin was in the world before the law was given, but sin is not charged against anyone's account where there is no law. ¹⁴Nevertheless, death reigned from the time of Adam to the time of Moses, even over those who did not sin by breaking a command, as did Adam, who is a pattern of the one to come.

¹⁵But the gift is not like the trespass. For if the many died by the trespass of the one man, how much more did God's grace and the gift that came by the grace of the one man, Jesus Christ, overflow to the many! ¹⁶Nor can the gift of God be compared with the result of one man's sin: The judgment followed one sin and brought condemnation, but the gift followed many trespasses and brought justification. ¹⁷For if, by the trespass of the one man, death reigned through that one man, how much more will those who receive God's abundant provision of grace and of the gift of righteousness reign in life through the one man, Jesus Christ!

¹⁸Consequently, just as one trespass resulted in condemnation for all people, so also one righteous act resulted in justification and life for all people. ¹⁹For just as through the disobedience of the one man the many were made sinners, so also through the obedience of the one man the many will be made righteous.

Devotion

We all love free, don't we? We can win the smallest little thing and be really excited about it. Even if the item is not something we want, we sometimes feel like victors just having won it! Today's scripture tells us of two freebies we've been given. The first is not so exciting. Through sin, Adam gave us death. He's the one who got us into this mess. Thank You, God, for having a better plan and getting us out of the mess.

Through His own death, Jesus gave us the most amazing free gift we will ever receive! In a single act, Jesus made available the gift of being made right with God to all of humanity. Now THAT is a free gift to get excited about! Scripture describes this gift as gracious, wonderful and eternal. Let that soak in, friends. You have been offered the gift of righteousness for doing absolutely nothing. This free gift offers you new life! You can live in triumph over sin and death because of this gift. It really sounds too simple. There is one catch. You have to obey God by accepting the gift. Maybe you did years ago. Or maybe for you, it was much more recently. Maybe it's something you need to do now.

Because one man—Jesus Christ—obeyed, many have been made righteous. While Jesus did that in a big way for all people in history, I wonder if He wants to do that in little ways in the present time in our lives. Because one man (YOUR NAME HERE) obeys, his family is being made righteous. Or because one woman (YOUR NAME HERE) obeys, her co-workers are being made righteous. Or because one man obeys, (YOUR NAME HERE) obeys and everyone around him is being made righteous. Those are statements I want to be said of me!

Thank You, Lord Jesus, that You have paved the way for us to have a right relationship with God. Help us to honor You each day by accepting Your amazing gift. May we obey You more and more with each passing day.

Reflection Questions

•How are you trying to earn justification and righteousness?

_____

_____

_____

_____

•What is one area of sin in your life that you need to call on God to help you live in triumph over?

_____

_____

_____

_____

•How are you doing at obeying God currently?

_____

WEEK 2 | DAY 5 | FRIDAY
Matthew 4:1-11 | Bonnie Hollabaugh

Matthew 4:1-11 (NIV)

[1]Then Jesus was led by the Spirit into the wilderness to be tempted by the devil. [2]After fasting forty days and forty nights, he was hungry. [3]The tempter came to him and said, "If you are the Son of God, tell these stones to become bread." [4]Jesus answered, "It is written: 'Man shall not live on bread alone, but on every word that comes from the mouth of God.'"

[5]Then the devil took him to the holy city and had him stand on the highest point of the temple. [6]"If you are the Son of God," he said, "throw yourself down. For it is written:

"'He will command his angels concerning you,
        and they will lift you up in their hands,
        so that you will not strike your foot against a stone.'"

[7]Jesus answered him, "It is also written: 'Do not put the Lord your God to the test.'"

[8]Again, the devil took him to a very high mountain and showed him all the kingdoms of the world and their splendor. [9]"All this I will give you," he said, "if you will bow down and worship me." [10]Jesus said to him, "Away from me, Satan! For it is written: 'Worship the Lord your God, and serve him only.'" [11]Then the devil left him, and angels came and attended him.

Thank You, Lord, for facing temptation so faithfully. Give us grace to do the same this day. I ask for Your strength to stand up to temptation whenever I encounter it. Please, Lord, give me the wisdom to walk away when I am tempted and the clarity to see the way out that You will provide. Amen.

Devotion

There is always the temptation to choose another way—a way that at the time seems more fun, an easy gain or just more satisfying or enjoyable. However, we are called to be obedient unto death. Temptation is defined as a trial or testing of one's faith—anything that draws us off our path of a true and righteous relationship with God.

- Do I want power to the point that I compromise my values or the reputation of a co-worker?

- Do I use drugs/liquor to cover my needs and try to ignore the possibility of addiction?

• Do I flirt much with my best friend's spouse to the point that it could lead to adultery?

• As a teen do I spend too much time alone with my honey that I am tempted to "go too far"?

• Do I alter my tax returns or financial reports such that it could become deceitful gain?

As long as we are in this world, we will be confronted with temptation. It touches each one of us. It touched Adam and Eve in the Garden; it touched Jesus. Being tempted is part of life and is not evil in and of itself. How we react to temptation is key! Temptation will come, and it can (and must!) be defeated.

Each one of us has had an experience where we had the awareness and alertness that we should do one thing, but we had the desire to choose another way—a way that would offer satisfaction or pleasure in the moment but not in the long run. Knowing these times and temptations will come, we must be filled with the Holy Spirit and the Word of God so that we will be reminded of our pact of obedience—our pact with God to pursue only those things that are holy and pleasing to Him.

Know that whatever temptation you face, you are not the first and you will not be the last to face that challenge. Don't be afraid to admit your struggles. When you are not prepared for it, it's easy to give in! We are most vulnerable when our guard is down. Know that God is always with us! He is faithful and trustworthy. Know that your brothers and sisters in Christ are by your side. The Holy Spirit is always with us! Have you ever been tempted to do something and right at that moment, the phone rings or there is some interruption that distracts you? That is the Holy Spirit. God does not tempt you. In fact He provides a way out!

Like everything in life, your actions are a choice. "The devil made me do it!" is not a valid excuse. He did not MAKE you do anything. You did it, and you are responsible for it. The devil may have tempted you, but YOU made the ultimate choice. Our failure to pursue the things of God has a profound impact on our relationship with God and with others. Let's devote ourselves to the pursuit of holy things!

Reflection Questions

• What are some ways God has helped you escape temptation?

_____

_____

•Think about a time when you were tempted to sin. How did you respond? What helped you or could have helped you resist the temptation?

_____

_____

_____

_____

•Have you ever been caught off guard by temptation?

_____

_____

_____

_____

SUNDAY

SHANE STANFORD

LUKE 19:1-10

Have you ever wondered what would cause Zacchaeus to make his way to the street? He was clearly not welcome as he weaved in and out of the crowds, trying to catch a glimpse of Jesus. And it wasn't just his physical stature that prevented him from getting close. The crowd despised Zacchaeus and anyone like him who, in their eyes, was defiling the faith—not to mention also taking their money. Zacchaeus was the worst kind of pariah—as a tax collector for Rome, his transgression was considered a betrayal of the core of Jewish culture.

As with so many stories in the Bible, the setting for Zacchaeus' encounter with Jesus is certainly no coincidence. Jericho has a familiar history—it was the ancient city that, centuries before, stood between the Israelites and the Promised Land. When Joshua arrived with the Israelites, Jericho was insulated, proud of its ability to keep out the unwanted. Its 'tumbling walls' became the stuff of legend—what child's Bible storybook doesn't include an account of Joshua and his army marching around the city until the walls collapsed upon themselves? The rest, as they say, is history.

By the time of Jesus, it had more than rebounded. Jericho had become a geographic and cultural center of the ancient world, considered a travel hub for getting to Jerusalem and other regions of Palestine. Because of this, trade and commerce thrived in Jericho, making it one of the wealthiest cities of the area and providing its inhabitants with high social status. The Romans valued Jericho because of its tax potential; thus, as a tax collector, Zacchaeus was not just any run-of-the-mill official—he was a prized part of the Roman establishment.

However, to the Jewish citizens of Jericho, Zacchaeus was a traitor. Sure, he had achieved great power and wealth, but at what price? He was one of the most hated men in the city, epitomizing the image of someone who possessed everything but had nothing. It was a life of great and painful contrasts: the best of the world's bounty, the worst of the soul's distress.

We know little about Zacchaeus' past, how he grew up or how he rose to the position of tax collector. What we do know is that Zacchaeus, for one reason or another, had chosen this life and, as is often the case with those like him, found himself in a pattern of choices that, over time, offered little in the way of better alternatives.

Still, Zacchaeus sought something different. Maybe he had heard about Jesus and His teachings, about how He loved the sinners and ate with outcasts. Something within Zacchaeus must have liked the idea of what Jesus stood for, and longed for the opportunity to know more about Him. We'll never know.

Regardless, we find Zacchaeus weaving through the hateful crowd, vying for an opportunity to see the Teacher from Nazareth. Zacchaeus determined that the risk was worth it, that maybe, unlike what everyone else in that crowd believed, he was not too far gone to change.

I believe that all of us, if we listen closely enough, can hear the ring of a new call in our lives. Very few of us get up in the morning, look in the mirror and say, "Today, I will screw up my life!" No, the voice deep within us, no matter how far we have wandered, echoes for new directions. So what is the problem? If the voice is speaking, why don't more of us listen and respond? Maybe it is a lack of courage, or perhaps fear of the unknown. Possibly it is just self-centeredness, the belief that we can or at least should be able to guide the journey ourselves. Or just maybe, we can't get our brains around the possibility that God could love us in this state—that God would accept us like this.

I'm sure Zacchaeus could never have imagined how his day would turn out. Who could? Getting a glimpse of Jesus is one thing; having Him invite Himself to dinner at your house? Whatever he was thinking that day, Zacchaeus did the only thing we are asked to do: He made his way to the street, broken life in hand, and waited to see if there was any truth to what he had heard about this Jesus.

Zacchaeus made his way to the street because he was tired of hurting. He was tired of knowing that no matter how many things he accumulated, he would still feel empty. Zacchaeus was sad about not knowing his neighbors and even sadder that his neighbors thought they knew him. His broken heart pushed him to the street hoping that on this day, just maybe something would give, and something in his life could change.

But getting to the street was only the beginning; he then had to fight his way through the crowd. Their anger was real. Zacchaeus knew he had helped plant it in their hearts. He was not innocent. The people had every right to hate him—and I'm sure the Adversary loved reminding him of that. But Zacchaeus kept walking, kept shouting back at the whisper of doubt inside him and kept looking through the crowd to see if Jesus had arrived.

At that moment, Zacchaeus must have felt hopeless. Soul weary. Human nature says, *Turn around. Why try? You'll never make it through the crowd. They won't let you!* But, then Zacchaeus saw the tree, and he began to climb. He climbed more quickly and farther than he could have imagined.

"If I wait for immaculate, I will never have a guest," writes Lauren F. Winner. Certainly Zacchaeus couldn't wait for immaculate, couldn't wait for everything to be perfect. Time was working against him, and the Guest was coming around the corner. So what if they made fun of him for climbing a tree to get a glimpse of Jesus? Zacchaeus knew the crowd would not miraculously part. No, this was as perfect as it would ever be.

When Jesus saw Zacchaeus sitting in the tree, He stopped and called him by name: "Zacchaeus, come down. Today, I will eat at your house" (see Luke 19:5). Can you imagine the shock, not only for Zacchaeus, but also for the entire crowd? *Did Jesus just speak to Zacchaeus? Did He just say that He was eating dinner at Zacchaeus' house?* I'm sure the questions and comments rivaled anything our modern gossip experts could generate.

But Jesus knew exactly what He was doing. Let's face it, Jesus is a "name-caller," and the name He likes the most is our own. Throughout the Gospels, we hear of Jesus calling people by name—and not just the religious folks, either. No, Jesus spent time calling the names of people who hadn't heard their names spoken in a welcoming tone in quite a while. Jesus knew the power of giving people dignity in order to later change their lives. It had probably been a long time since someone had called Zacchaeus by name without connecting it to some form of profanity or curse. To hear his name spoken by Jesus, of all people, must have been like hearing beautiful music.

However, Jesus is not only a name-caller. He also likes a good party. We know because He was always inviting Himself to one. And why not? What better place to get to know someone than around a table, sharing a good meal with good friends? Jesus liked to enter into people's space and get to the heart of who they were. He couldn't have cared less about what the religious folks and the social elite thought. Jesus wanted to know the real insides of people so that He could fill those empty places with something of real value.

By calling Zacchaeus' name, Jesus gave Zacchaeus an identity; by going to his home, Jesus gave Zacchaeus a future. Jesus placed a name on the pile of debris called Zacchaeus' life and gave meaning to it all.

Zacchaeus' response surprised those around him, but it shouldn't surprise us. We read the rest of the story and know what happens when sinners encounter the love of Jesus: The change can't be contained. It is overwhelming, and it causes people to do crazy things, like give away their possessions and try to make things right. Zacchaeus did the only thing he could have done. His heart had been opened and he wanted to respond, but not in some token way.

No, Zacchaeus exploded in gratitude and thanksgiving. He gave back to those who he had wronged, not once or twice but four times what he owed them. Forgiveness makes people do amazing things because forgiveness is in itself such an amazing act—and the more amazing it feels, the more amazing the response.

Even more wonderful, though, was Jesus' proclamation. After Zacchaeus responded, Jesus declared, "Today, salvation has come to this house, because this man, too, is a son of Abraham" (Luke 19:9). Jesus named Zacchaeus and restored him to the family. Zacchaeus was no longer an outcast or orphan; he belonged. Why did he belong? Because of a profound truth in Jesus' final statement, words that speak to every Zacchaeus everywhere who believes that his or her life has too much baggage for God to ever love him or her. Jesus looked at those gathered around that table and said, "For the Son of Man came to seek and to save what was lost" (Luke 19:10).

Think about that for a minute. Did you hear those two words? *Seek and save.* Zacchaeus had never been too far gone or too hopeless to find the love of God. And God didn't want Zacchaeus to miss out on the sweetness of a transformed life.

God is there, seeking after us, guiding us and showing us the way. We may not see or even know it, but God is always watching and waiting. How, you ask? Think about how Jesus found Zacchaeus. Was it a coincidence that the sycamore tree was there so that a vertically challenged tax collector, hated by a crowd that would never let him pass, could climb and be seen? And was it a coincidence that the same tree provided a platform so that when Jesus called Zacchaeus' name, Zacchaeus was more than front and center: He was up and in view of the One who longed to meet with him? I don't believe in coincidences. God seeks what is lost—always has, always will—and that means He will use anything to reach us if we are willing to trust and believe.

God doesn't stop there. Not only does He *seek* the lost, God also *saves* the lost. This wasn't—and isn't—a game for Jesus. The wee little man in the sycamore tree might make for great Bible songs and rhymes, but for Zacchaeus, and those like him, it isn't a game, either. It means everything. God's goal in drawing close to us through Jesus is not just that we might know our sin, but also that God might transform our lives and make us new in the midst of that sin. Calling Zacchaeus by name was one thing; changing his heart and life . . . well, that was a miracle.

Friend, let's stop making excuses for living in the filth. Let's stop thinking of everyone we can blame, and take some responsibility for where our lives have landed. It's trash-bagging time and, believe me, we will not regret it. The sorrow of past mistakes and bad choices needs to be thrown to the curb so that someone much more capable than we can haul it away and give us something new.

Okay, so we might have to climb a tree or two.

We may get a few bruises, scrapes and cuts along the way, but we won't let that stop us. In fact, we'll name them. We'll call them swallowing our pride, letting go of our shame, forgetting our pain, getting out of our own way.

And I have some great news for you: While you are busy naming the things that have held you back, done you in or beaten you down, God will be calling your name. And you will never be the same again. Jesus is coming to your house today!

Reflection Questions

The story of Zacchaeus is familiar, possibly too familiar. Many times, we focus on the children's version with the "wee little man in a tree," and we miss Zacchaeus' heart-wrenching search for peace with God and his neighbors. This lesson highlights both personal responsibility and God's faithfulness to accept and respond to our lives wherever He might find us. As we navigate through our own spiritual crowd, we feel Zacchaeus' feelings of rejection, shame and guilt as all too familiar.

The Bible says, *"Come near to God and he will come near to you"* (James 4:8).

•Make a list of the broken areas in your life that need to be packed up and taken to the street.

_____

_____

_____

_____

_____

_____

•How do your broken places keep you from seeking God in your life?

_____

_____

_____

_____

•What are you willing to do in order to catch a glimpse of Jesus? What keeps you from acting on it?

_____

_____

_____

Week 3 | Day 1 | Monday
Genesis 3:1-13 | Mike Weaver

Father, help us to confess our sin and rebellion before You, so that whenever and wherever You call out, "Where are you?" we say, "Here I am, Lord!" Amen.

Genesis 3:1-13 (NIV)

¹Now the serpent was more crafty than any of the wild animals the Lord God had made. He said to the woman, "Did God really say, 'You must not eat from any tree in the garden'?"

²The woman said to the serpent, "We may eat fruit from the trees in the garden, ³but God did say, 'You must not eat fruit from the tree that is in the middle of the garden, and you must not touch it, or you will die.'"

⁴"You will not certainly die," the serpent said to the woman. ⁵"For God knows that when you eat from it your eyes will be opened, and you will be like God, knowing good and evil."

⁶When the woman saw that the fruit of the tree was good for food and pleasing to the eye, and also desirable for gaining wisdom, she took some and ate it. She also gave some to her husband, who was with her, and he ate it. ⁷Then the eyes of both of them were opened, and they realized they were naked; so they sewed fig leaves together and made coverings for themselves.

⁸Then the man and his wife heard the sound of the Lord God as he was walking in the garden in the cool of the day, and they hid from the Lord God among the trees of the garden. ⁹But the Lord God called to the man, "Where are you?"

¹⁰He answered, "I heard you in the garden, and I was afraid because I was naked; so I hid."

¹¹And he said, "Who told you that you were naked? Have you eaten from the tree that I commanded you not to eat from?"

¹²The man said, "The woman you put here with me—she gave me some fruit from the tree, and I ate it."

¹³Then the Lord God said to the woman, "What is this you have done?"

The woman said, "The serpent deceived me, and I ate."

Devotion

God asked Adam a very important question. "Adam, where are you?" If you have been in church very long, you probably have been taught that God is omniscient, all knowing. God asked Adam the question so Adam would realize where he was. God already knew, but He wanted Adam to know that something was wrong, tragically wrong—something terrible had happened. Adam and Eve had sinned, and with that sin there were consequences.

The radical change within their hearts and minds was traumatic. Their hearts and minds had never known anything but perfection. But now their sin had changed all that. Adam and Eve stood there, having just sinned, stripped of all the perfection and innocence of their being. They knew—sensed and felt within their minds and hearts—that they were naked. The clothing of their perfection and innocence was now stripped away. They had perfect control, discipline and obedience, but sin made them feel guilt and shame.

So now there is a question for you and me because of Adam. "Where are you?" First Corinthians 15:22 says, "For as in Adam all die..." The scripture tells us we are now all sinners. Romans 5:12 says, "Therefore, just as sin entered the world through one man, and death through sin, and in this way death came to all people, because all sinned." The Bible teaches that the payment for sin is death (Romans 6:23).

We know the consequences of sin, but is there a cure? Praise the Lord, yes. In that very same chapter in Genesis, God gives us a glimpse into the glory that is to come. "And I will put enmity between you and the woman, and between your offspring and hers;
he will crush your head, and you will strike his heel" (Genesis 3:15). God is making reference to the One to come, the One mentioned in 1 Corinthians 15:22.

How? Romans 5:8-9 says, "But God demonstrates his own love for us in this: While we were still sinners, Christ died for us. Since we have now been justified by his blood, how much more shall we be saved from God's wrath through him!"

What does this word "blood" mean? It speaks to me of the death of Christ and tells me there is nothing I can do about getting myself right with God. The work has been finished by Jesus. There is something about the nature of sin and about the nature of God that required a plan to deal with man's sin. And the cross tells me that it has been done. Are you prepared to accept the fact that Christ has atoned for sin and God doesn't expect you to do it?

Reflection Questions

• Is there a place in your life where God is calling out to you saying, "Where are you right now with_____"? Is there a thing or a sin you have been hiding from God for too long that you need to confess? Write it down.

_____

_____

_____

_____

• What are some things you're tangibly doing to remind yourself that God has already won redemption for you, and you don't have to win it on your own?

_____

_____

_____

_____

• How are you planning to practically respond *today* to the fact that God has won forgiveness for you in Christ?

_____

_____

_____

_____

Lord, thank You for Your sustaining grace. Forgive me for the times I am tempted to think You have forgotten me. Restore within me a settled assurance that You will take care of me and the ones I love. Help me believe this so strongly that I will choose to no longer worry but sing praises to You. Amen.

Psalm 121 (NIV)

> ^{1}I lift up my eyes to the mountains—
> where does my help come from?
> ^{2}My help comes from the Lord,
> the Maker of heaven and earth.
> ^{3}He will not let your foot slip—
> he who watches over you will not slumber;
> ^{4}indeed, he who watches over Israel
> will neither slumber nor sleep.
> ^{5}The Lord watches over you—
> the Lord is your shade at your right hand;
> ^{6}the sun will not harm you by day,
> nor the moon by night.
> ^{7}The Lord will keep you from all harm—
> he will watch over your life;
> ^{8}the Lord will watch over your coming and going
> both now and forevermore.

Devotion

Our doorbell rang late one afternoon. I answered to find our nearly 90-year-old neighbor, Mr. Bailey, grinning from ear to ear. Wow, did he have a story to tell! A men's clothing store in the town he had worked for many years was preparing for its 50th anniversary. The celebration included offering a brand new suit to the customer who brought in the oldest suit bought from them. Mr. Bailey had carefully kept and cared for his half-century old suit purchased the same year the store opened. He won the prize and left the store with both his old suit and his new one!

Some things are worth keeping! That's what God thinks of His people. Say it with me, "God thinks I'm a keeper!" Psalm 121 recounts God's extraordinary preservation of those who seek Him and love Him. Six times in eight verses we find the word "keep." Some versions translate it three times as "preserve," but it is the same word. The Israelites, journeying from different lands toward Jerusalem, faced many potential hazards—many miles, bad weather, robbery, wildlife attack and slithering serpents, not to mention hunger, thirst and bleeding blisters. The journey was hard and called for great praise every time it was finished. The first glimpse of the mountains as God's people drew near their beloved city started them singing, "The Lord is your keeper" (Psalm 121:5, NKJV).

The Christian journey is not an easy life either, but it is a cared for life. God doesn't throw us away or turn away from us when life becomes difficult. He watches over us, cares for us, preserves us and sustains us by His grace. He keeps us. To be kept is to be cared for!

One day God will take us safely home to heaven. When He does, we will know the joy of exchanging our old suit for a new one.

Reflection Questions

•How did God care for you during a difficult time? Remember and give thanks.

_____

_____

_____

_____

•What is the greatest present concern in your life?

_____

_____

_____

_____

•Will you trust God to care for you?

_____

_____

_____

_____

Gracious God, we know that we are unable to perfectly keep Your law. And we know that when we break Your laws, we break Your heart. Forgive us. Break our pride so that we can take You completely at Your word. We want to receive Your righteousness and then live it. Thank You for Abraham who showed us the way. Thank You, God, thank You. In Jesus' holy name we pray, Amen.

Romans 4:1-5, 13-17 (NIV)

¹What then shall we say that Abraham, our forefather according to the flesh, discovered in this matter? ²If, in fact, Abraham was justified by works, he had something to boast about—but not before God. ³What does Scripture say? "Abraham believed God, and it was credited to him as righteousness."
⁴Now to the one who works, wages are not credited as a gift but as an obligation. ⁵However, to the one who does not work but trusts God who justifies the ungodly, their faith is credited as righteousness.

***

¹³It was not through the law that Abraham and his offspring received the promise that he would be heir of the world, but through the righteousness that comes by faith. ¹⁴For if those who depend on the law are heirs, faith means nothing and the promise is worthless, ¹⁵because the law brings wrath. And where there is no law there is no transgression. ¹⁶Therefore, the promise comes by faith, so that it may be by grace and may be guaranteed to all Abraham's offspring—not only to those who are of the law but also to those who have the faith of Abraham. He is the father of us all. ¹⁷As it is written: "I have made you a father of many nations." He is our father in the sight of God, in whom he believed—the God who gives life to the dead and calls into being things that were not.

Devotion
How in the world do we really define faith? Imagine you were Abraham of the Old Testament: very elderly, you had no children and the God of the universe Himself appeared and spoke directly to you. He said that you would not only father children, but would have as many descendants as the stars themselves. Would you believe Him? Strange as that might have sounded to us or to Abraham, he *took God at His word*. And in that very act, God in return reckoned him as righteous. A cleansed slate, making it possible to actually stand blameless before God Almighty, with absolutely nothing written in a ledger of wrongdoings. An incomprehensible grace gift! Renamed as righteous, justified, an heir to the Kingdom, God's forever Kingdom.

We are such "doers," justifying our own existence, working to win God's approval and love. It's hard to grasp that even in our greatest frenzy of performing wonderful deeds for Him, there is *nothing* we can do or offer to God to be good enough to deserve and earn His love. It's not by works. It's not faith *plus* anything else. It's faith. Period! It's doing the very simple thing that God requires, emptying our hands and humbly accepting the gift by taking God at His word. E. Stanley Jones said, "With the gift of righteousness, the emphasis is not on my guilt, but upon His goodness." Me, righteous? You, righteous? God says YES! And I believe it.

But what about those good works? They continue, but instead of our straining to earn God's love, now they are a way of thanking God for His grace, telling the story to others, that they, too, can stand righteous in His presence. God said, "I AM THAT I AM." And our response? To take Him at His word, be renamed as righteous and serve Him through faith.

Reflection Questions

•Why is it so hard to do something so simple, to submit and receive the gift?

_____

_____

_____

_____

•Have you been renamed as an heir of God because of your faith?

_____

_____

_____

_____

•Can you name others with whom to share this remarkable story? Everybody needs to hear the Good News.

_____

_____

Almighty Father, You call me not to be a better person but to become a new person. I ask for the gift of faith to become new in You, for the gift of obedience to live out Your grace in every way and for the gift of love by which You come to save the whole world through Jesus Christ our Lord, Amen.

John 3:1-17 (NRSV)

[1]Now there was a Pharisee named Nicodemus, a leader of the Jews. [2]He came to Jesus by night and said to him, "Rabbi, we know that you are a teacher who has come from God; for no one can do these signs that you do apart from the presence of God." [3]Jesus answered him, "Very truly, I tell you, no one can see the kingdom of God without being born from above." [4]Nicodemus said to him, "How can anyone be born after having grown old? Can one enter a second time into the mother's womb and be born?" [5]Jesus answered, "Very truly, I tell you, no one can enter the kingdom of God without being born of water and Spirit. [6]What is born of the flesh is flesh, and what is born of the Spirit is spirit. [7]Do not be astonished that I said to you, 'You must be born from above.' [8]The wind blows where it chooses, and you hear the sound of it, but you do not know where it comes from or where it goes. So it is with everyone who is born of the Spirit." [9]Nicodemus said to him, "How can these things be?" [10]Jesus answered him, "Are you a teacher of Israel, and yet you do not understand these things?

[11]"Very truly, I tell you, we speak of what we know and testify to what we have seen; yet you do not receive our testimony. [12]If I have told you about earthly things and you do not believe, how can you believe if I tell you about heavenly things? [13]No one has ascended into heaven except the one who descended from heaven, the Son of Man. [14]And just as Moses lifted up the serpent in the wilderness, so must the Son of Man be lifted up, [15]that whoever believes in him may have eternal life.

[16]"For God so loved the world that he gave his only Son, so that everyone who believes in him may not perish but may have eternal life.

[17]"Indeed, God did not send the Son into the world to condemn the world, but in order that the world might be saved through him.

Devotion

Nicodemus is a human being who comes to Jesus at night.

At this point in the story, John has already dropped two clues about what this story is going to involve. He has just told us that many believe because of Jesus' miraculous signs but that Jesus knows everything about what is in a human (*anthropos*), and so He doesn't fully trust their ability to understand who He is and what He means for their lives (John 2:23-25).

Then suddenly, Nicodemus is introduced to us as one of these human beings—literally, "an *anthropos* of the Pharisees." We already assume, therefore, that as a human being Jesus is going to have special insight about Nicodemus' faith. And, as John points out, he comes to Jesus at *night*. The motif of darkness in his Gospel often symbolizes a lack of understanding or even opposition to Jesus—the opposite of faith (John 1:5; 13:30).

What does Nicodemus need to do in light of his very human problem that prevents him from experiencing the reign of God as it is now here in Jesus?

As Jesus tells him, he needs to be born *anothen*. The word can mean "from above" or simply "again," and Jesus is playing on the word by using it in both senses. However, Nicodemus appears to receive only the latter meaning, and Jesus wants him to understand the other, greater meaning—Nicodemus needs to be born not just a second time; he needs to be born of God.

So Jesus issues another wordplay to help Nicodemus arrive at his own understanding. The words *pneuma* and *phonē* can have two meanings—so is Jesus talking about the sound of the wind or the voice of the Spirit? Both! Jesus uses His language to invite Nicodemus to realize that the answer to his human problem of understanding is to embrace the salvation of God found in Him by heeding the voice of his Spirit. He in turn truly understands what Jesus is saying: He needs to be born again, but this second birth is a birth from above.

Like one's first birth, this second birth leads unto life, but what Jesus offers the believer through His exaltation on the cross is *eternal* life. And this life does not wait for us after death; it is given to us now, as we become a new people with a new origin and a new destiny.

Like Nicodemus, come to Jesus, the one who knows you—even in the night of your lack of faith and in the darkness of your opposition to God. Be born of Him, so that you may live for Him. Live for Him, so that you may become new in Him. Believe in Him, so that you may be saved through Him.

Reflection Questions

•What does it mean to you that Jesus truly understands what it means to be human? What difference does this make in how we relate to Him?

_____

_____

_____

_____

•What does it mean for you to be *born* of God? Why is this word used for what must happen for us to experience the kingdom of God? Why is it necessary for us to become new people, and how does this relate to the death that we are also called to experience as believers in Christ?

_____

_____

_____

_____

•What is the difference between condemnation and salvation? How do we know that Jesus came to save and not to condemn?

_____

_____

_____

_____

Dear Lord, You have opened the eyes of my heart to your wonderful plans for me. You have used the events of the day when Jesus stood with Moses and Elijah and became glorified. You do not give us Your Word so that it will be returned void. It comes to us with a purpose. Just as You came to us with a price, we honor You for the sacrifice that You made and the examples You have given us through these disciples and their faithfulness, even to death. Thank You for changing me and us from the inside so that we can be Your hands and feet on the outside. Amen.

Matthew 17:1-9 (NIV)

¹After six days Jesus took with him Peter, James and John the brother of James, and led them up a high mountain by themselves. ²There he was transfigured before them. His face shone like the sun, and his clothes became as white as the light. ³Just then there appeared before them Moses and Elijah, talking with Jesus.
⁴Peter said to Jesus, "Lord, it is good for us to be here. If you wish, I will put up three shelters—one for you, one for Moses and one for Elijah."
⁵While he was still speaking, a bright cloud covered them, and a voice from the cloud said, "This is my Son, whom I love; with him I am well pleased. Listen to him!"
⁶When the disciples heard this, they fell facedown to the ground, terrified. ⁷But Jesus came and touched them. "Get up," he said. "Don't be afraid." ⁸When they looked up, they saw no one except Jesus.
⁹As they were coming down the mountain, Jesus instructed them, "Don't tell anyone what you have seen, until the Son of Man has been raised from the dead."

Devotion

Up to the point of the Transfiguration, the disciples were probably of the belief that they were to be big beneficiaries of their association with Jesus. In fact, there is ample evidence that they had no inkling of the costs involved. But in Matthew 16, Jesus begins to question them by saying, "Who do you say I am?" (Matt. 16:15, NIV) Finally Peter says, "You are the Christ, the Son of the living God" (Matt. 16:16, ESV). And Jesus tells him that he is correct. But He also begins to tell them that it will cost them greatly, possibly everything they have and that only some will be in His presence before their lives end. In this chapter Jesus is called to explain to the Pharisees who He is, and, in turn, the disciples are also wondering what/who they have before them.

Reflection Questions

•What is "the Christ" Peter refers to in Matthew 16:16, and how is this distinct from "the Jesus" we know as a man sent from God but who IS God? Hint: one is our spiritual leader who unites and restores our soul from eternity back to our Father in heaven, and the other is the example here on earth of a perfect life.

_____

_____

_____

_____

_____

_____

•The appearance of Moses and Elijah on the Mount gives us a picture of eternity and of the existence of our spiritual certainty modeled in that encounter. Moses represents the covenant between God and His people sealed with the blood of the lamb—pointing to the ultimate sacrifice of the Son of Man. And Elijah represents prophesies that are to soon (six days) be fulfilled in the death and Resurrection. These three disciples with Jesus constituted the necessary quorum of three witnesses and were capable of carrying the messages forward that a) Jesus was the goal the law and prophets led to and b) not to confuse Jesus with either Moses or Elijah. They were servants too who were called out to serve a living God (just like us, Ekklesia, called out).

So, why did Jesus not have **all** the disciples witness the Transfiguration? See the last sentence above, and add any other thoughts you may have, such as the significance of Peter and his role in starting the Church or that maybe we need to 'see' them to model for the others (and us) how to explain the meaning of these events. In so doing, we learn that God trusted only them to get it right. Maybe He only trusts me or you with a real world explanation of His truth shared with someone else.

_____

_____

_____

_____

•Peter is having trouble understanding the significance of this heavenly encounter. He wants to erect some tents. Peter has trouble giving up the old ways of the Hebrews. He thinks God desires to be put back into the Tabernacle. He fails to see the role that the Christ will play from now on will be to live in and inhabit our souls. The new 'temple' will be Christ—in us! Why does Peter think to erect tents? Hint: What does the phrase "Christ in us, the hope of glory" (Colossians 1:27) mean to you?

_____

_____

_____

_____

_____

_____

_____

_____

SUNDAY

SHANE STANFORD

JOHN 4:1-42

As Jesus sat down beside the well, He rested. Jesus was thirsty and tired from a long day's journey. Like any traveler, He needed the basics to keep Him strong and healthy. And, so, as many times before, He stopped at a well for a drink. Leaving Jesus, the disciples went ahead to find food and water.

Also at the well was a Samaritan woman. The two words together—"Samaritan" and "woman"—spoke volumes about how and why Jesus, or any religious teacher, should have shunned her. Rabbinic law frowned upon men and women interacting in Jesus' day. But for a *Jewish* man to be seen in the company of a *Samaritan* woman was an abomination.

Samaritans were the offspring of the Assyrian conquerors who had shared relations with women from the 10 northern tribes of Israel. The direct descendants of the northern tribes were no more, but the symbol of the destruction of Assyria's invasion lived on in the Samaritans. They served as a living reminder to the Jews of the physical, geographical and religious domination laid on them and their land for centuries. And as mixed-race children, Samaritans were an affront to Jewish rules of purity and clean bloodlines. The Jews and the Samaritans had a long, unhappy history—a history that neither race seemed destined to forget.

The passage in John's Gospel implies that the woman at the well had other problems apart from her gender and nationality. First, she came to *this* particular well. Certainly there were wells closer to the town where she lived. But still she came to this site, remote and set apart from the village. This was a traveler's well, not the place where villagers would have come to draw their water.

Second, the Scripture tells us that the woman came to the well at the sixth hour. The Jewish day ran from 6 A.M. to 6 P.M. The sixth hour would have been exactly Noon, one of the hottest times of the day. Everyone would have known better than to be at the well at midday; people didn't draw water at that time—it was too hot and deserted. But maybe that was the whole point.

Let's think a minute. The woman travels past the bounds of her village (probably passing other wells on the way) to draw water, and she does so at the warmest part of the day. I don't know about you, but to me she sounds like a person who went out of her way to not encounter others. On most days, I'm sure the plan would have worked beautifully. But as we see so often with Jesus, all plans are subject to change.

One other thing . . . we shouldn't miss what the setting and timeframe say about Jesus. Why did He wait here while His disciples went into town for food? Why was He traveling in the heat of the day? Was Jesus' weariness just physical, or did He need a little alone time, too? The second lesson is found in how Jesus meets the woman at a point where her problems are reparable. Nothing in His demeanor or words suggests that her life or situation was beyond repair. Jesus met her with a straightforward approach. He didn't make her become something she wasn't in order to help her. Jesus never tried to console her in her troubles. And He never condemned her for her bad choices. Instead, Jesus offered her a realistic appraisal of her situation and then provided a solution: the truth.

The Adversary only needs to convince us that the lie is inevitable, or the only option, in order to stop us in our tracks. Mary had almost convinced herself that her life would consist of one broken path after another, that she was doomed to some perpetual pattern of emptiness. The woman at the well believed her thirst could never be filled, except by bad choices, out-of-the-way relationships and less-than-fresh water.

But encountering the truth means seeing that our thirst doesn't have to last forever. Told correctly and honestly, the truth, in whatever form God unveils it to us, simply states the facts—it doesn't play favorites, judge or condemn. And, in that moment, the truth becomes our greatest tool for finding real life in Christ.

Reflection Questions

Inward shame breeds outward attitude, or at least it did for the woman at the well. In this encounter, Jesus confronted human need at its deepest soul-tearing level, and the woman, an outcast from her own people, discovered her faith in Jesus' discovery of her. She also realized that removing the barrier between "good religion" and real faith begins with a recognition that there are some needs no worldly relationship can meet. Jesus quenched a thirst the woman was afraid to admit she had. The woman exposed the dry, cracked places of fear, guilt and doubt that gnawed within her and drank from a grace that promised to never leave her thirsty again.

The Bible says to present ourselves as "holy and living sacrifices" (Romans 12:1), but we contaminate our lives with bitterness, bad decisions and wasted opportunities. List those areas of bitterness or regret that keep you from seeing God in your daily life.

_____

_____

_____

_____

_____

What keeps those places so raw and unhealed?

_____

_____

_____

_____

Do you celebrate God knowing everything about you? Why or why not?

_____

_____

_____

_____

_____

Jesus purifies our lives with grace, restoration and hope. Name your blessings (one by one, if you can) through which God speaks to the deepest places of your soul and gives you hope.

_____

_____

_____

_____

_____

_____

_____

_____

Lord, quench my thirst with Your presence. Guard my heart from discontent. Keep me from testing You, from quarrelling with You. Help me, my Deliverer and Provider, to follow You through the wilderness of my days with unwavering faith in Your provisions and love for me, knowing that all my thirsts and hungers are actually desires for You. Amen.

Exodus 17:1-7 (NIV)

[1]The whole Israelite community set out from the Desert of Sin, traveling from place to place as the Lord commanded. They camped at Rephidim, but there was no water for the people to drink. [2]So they quarreled with Moses and said, "Give us water to drink."

Moses replied, "Why do you quarrel with me? Why do you put the Lord to the test?"

[3]But the people were thirsty for water there, and they grumbled against Moses. They said, "Why did you bring us up out of Egypt to make us and our children and livestock die of thirst?"

[4]Then Moses cried out to the Lord, "What am I to do with these people? They are almost ready to stone me."

[5]The Lord answered Moses, "Go out in front of the people. Take with you some of the elders of Israel and take in your hand the staff with which you struck the Nile, and go. [6]I will stand there before you by the rock at Horeb. Strike the rock, and water will come out of it for the people to drink." So Moses did this in the sight of the elders of Israel. [7]And he called the place Massah and Meribah because the Israelites quarreled and because they tested the Lord saying, "Is the Lord among us or not?"

Devotion

Unquenched spiritual thirst leads to a quarrelsome, discontent soul. That is certainly one of the clearest lessons from Exodus 17:1-7, where we find the newly delivered, but now discontent, Israel quarreling with and testing God. Israel's wilderness wandering brought them to Rephidim, a dry area with no available water to drink. The Israelites, parched and wander-weary, allowed their thirst to reduce them to a people depleted of hope and void of trust in their God of deliverance. Days on days of trekking through the wilderness created unrest in the community of God's people, while worsening physical thirst calloused their hearts against Moses to the point that the people wanted to stone him! (Exodus 17:4) And from their hardened hearts and parched mouths Israel contentiously cried, "Give us water to drink!"

It only takes a casual reading of Exodus to realize that Israel's demand is not purely physical. From their first steps out of bondage in Egypt, Israel revealed themselves to be an ungrateful, complaining people, despite God's continual goodness to them. It is just one chapter before, in Exodus 16, that the Lord pours provisions on His people through the daily bread of manna and quail and so demonstrates that He is a God who meets needs.

And it is just a short time before the grumblings of Exodus 17 that God miraculously delivers Israel, as they stand on the verge of being crushed between the sea and the forces of Pharaoh. Yet regardless of God's saving interventions, Exodus 17 opens with an astonishing but far too frequent scene: Israel thanklessly, forgetfully, neglectfully complaining to God.

What is God's response to His people's grumblings? He quenches their physical thirst and seeks to fill their spiritual void. God, from His invincible mercy, instructs Moses to strike the rock at Horeb, from which water will then flow to nourish the Israelites. This amazing physical provision points to a greater spiritual truth. The most remarkable truth in this scene is that in meeting Israel's physical needs, God is revealing His desire to fill their spiritual void.

Amazingly, what Yahweh does for Israel in Exodus 17, Jesus ultimately does for humanity. Nowhere is Jesus' invitation for those thirsty to be filled with His presence better demonstrated than in John 7:37-38, "If anyone thirsts, let him come to me and drink. Whoever believes in me, as Scripture has said, 'Out of his heart will flow rivers of living water.'" (ESV)

We are a thirsty people. It only takes our wandering hearts to meet unfavorable life circumstances for our thirst to reveal our grumbling, testing, quarrelsome spirits. Yet God gives us the water of His presence. God, through Christ, desires that the living water of His spirit not flow from any rock, but from our very hearts. May we be a people of contentment. May we live in thirst for His presence. May we be a people whose thirst is quenched from the rock of Jesus.

Reflection Questions

•A major theme in scripture is that "man should not live by bread alone." Do you find that your physical desires or problems take prominence over your spiritual thirst?

• Practically speaking, how can you guard against the testing and quarreling that so characterized Israel?

_____

_____

_____

_____

• When reading the Old Testament, it is important to always look for connections to the New Testament, such as the connection between Exodus 17:1-7 and John 7:37-38. Take some time to read the entire book of Exodus. What other connections do you see between it and the New Testament?

_____

_____

_____

_____

Lord, we confess that we are prideful. Bowing down is not our regular stance. Save us from thinking more highly of ourselves than we ought to think, from thinking we are sufficient within ourselves. Give us the grace to be completely Yours that we might sing with joy, no matter what is happening on our journey. Amen.

Psalm 95 (NIV)

¹Come, let us sing for joy to the LORD;
   let us shout aloud to the Rock of our salvation.
²Let us come before him with thanksgiving

   and extol him with music and song.

³For the LORD is the great God,

   the great King above all gods.
⁴In his hand are the depths of the earth,

   and the mountain peaks belong to him.
⁵The sea is his, for he made it,

   and his hands formed the dry land.

⁶Come, let us bow down in worship,

   let us kneel before the LORD our Maker;
⁷for he is our God

   and we are the people of his pasture,

   the flock under his care.

 Today, if only you would hear his voice,
⁸"Do not harden your hearts as you did at Meribah,

   as you did that day at Massah in the wilderness,
⁹where your ancestors tested me;

   they tried me, though they had seen what I did.
¹⁰For forty years I was angry with that generation;

   I said, 'They are a people whose hearts go astray,

and they have not known my ways.'
¹¹So I declared on oath in my anger,

'They shall never enter my rest.'"

Devotion

Our temptation as we read this psalm is to concentrate on the first verses. "Come, let us sing for joy to the LORD; let us shout aloud to the Rock of our salvation." Yes, yes!

"Come before him with thanksgiving and extol him with music and song." Yes, yes!

We like it—nothing demanding.

But then in verse 6, the mood changes, "Come, let us bow down...kneel before the Lord our Maker." Bow down? Are we talking about recognizing who is really in charge? Admitting that we can't do it on our own?

In verses 8-11, the psalmist goes back in history. Israel, chosen by God and delivered from Egypt, crossed over the Red Sea and spent 40 years in the wilderness of the Exodus. They interpreted that 40 years as a time of testing and temptation.

The reference to Meribah and Massah comes from when they arrived in Rephidim (Exodus 17). There was no water, and they began to quarrel and accuse Moses of bringing them out to die. The psalmist pleads on behalf of God, "Do not harden your hearts as you did at Meribah and Massah." Meribah means quarreling; Massah means testing.

In this story, the Israelites are journeying, as is the church. Israel's story is our story. She has been redeemed out of slavery in Egypt, just as we have been redeemed by the cross and resurrection of Jesus Christ out of our slavery to sin and death. Now, like Israel, we are making our way through the wilderness toward a promised land. We are on the way between our redemption and our final salvation in the Kingdom of God. We are too far along now to turn back or miss the way.

Reflection Questions

•What is preventing you from singing for joy to the Lord today?

_____

_____

•What would have to change in your life for you to genuinely bow down?

_____

_____

_____

_____

_____

• What do you need to add to your spiritual disciplines to get the most out of this Lenten season?

_____

_____

_____

_____

God of peace, thank You for the grace, hope and love found through Your Son. Thank You for the grace in which I securely stand. Thank You for a hope that can I place in Your eternal glory that surpasses the hardships of this temporal life. Thank You for the love that You have poured into my heart. Help me to live out the justification I have in Your sacrifice. Help me to live continually in faith. Amen.

Romans 5:1-11

[1]Therefore, since we have been justified through faith, we have peace with God through our Lord Jesus Christ, [2]through whom we have gained access by faith into this grace in which we now stand. And we boast in the hope of the glory of God. [3]Not only so, but we also glory in our sufferings, because we know that suffering produces perseverance; [4]perseverance, character; and character, hope. [5]And hope does not put us to shame, because God's love has been poured out into our hearts through the Holy Spirit, who has been given to us.

[6]You see, at just the right time, when we were still powerless, Christ died for the ungodly. [7]Very rarely will anyone die for a righteous person, though for a good person someone might possibly dare to die. [8]But God demonstrates his own love for us in this: While we were still sinners, Christ died for us.

[9]Since we have now been justified by his blood, how much more shall we be saved from God's wrath through him! [10]For if, while we were God's enemies, we were reconciled to him through the death of his Son, how much more, having been reconciled, shall we be saved through his life! [11]Not only is this so, but we also boast in God through our Lord Jesus Christ, through whom we have now received reconciliation.

Devotion

The Epistle to the Romans is Paul's most elaborate explanation of justification through faith in Christ. In addressing a Christian community in Rome complexly divided between Jews and Gentiles, all once alienated from God in their sin, Paul paints a portrait of Christ's atoning death bringing reconciliatory peace between God and humanity and instills hope in our hearts.

One of the most powerful passages of Romans, if not all of the New Testament, Romans 5:1-5 describes the overwhelming blessings we have in Christ, blessings heaped onto us through justification through Christ. Justification, a legal term that

Paul frequently used in his letters, connotes the act of God declaring those who believe in Christ guiltless and innocent before Him. Through faith in Christ alone we are moved from a state of isolation from God into a union of peace, grace and hope with God through Jesus. The profoundly powerful truth that the justifying work of Christ has given us peace with God—"we have peace with God through our Lord Jesus Christ. Through Him we have also obtained access by faith into this grace in which we stand"(Romans 5:1-2)—creates in us an unflappable, assured hope that gives us the ability to rejoice in our sufferings. Rejoicing—not merely enduring, as we so often think suffering should be handled—in hardship is here a part of this grander work of justification that births this Christ-centered hope.

So often we fail to believe in and take hold of this great hope in Christ, do we not? Our sufferings cloud our hope. Our hardships, if allowed, deny the glory we owe God. And sadly, far too often we fail to live in light of the peace and grace that gives us such hope. Paul's message is meant to shore up that hope in our hearts. We have peace because of our faith in Christ. We have faith because of God's gracious love for us. We know grace through the Holy Spirit's indwelling in our hearts. And we can live in a hope that transcends the shame of even the most extreme suffering because God through Christ has declared us innocent. One great lesson from Romans 5 is that justification through Christ has changed everything for us. No longer separated from God in sin, we live as a people justified by grace through faith with an eternal hope in our hearts.

Take heart, saints. Have faith. Enjoy peace. Stand in grace. Walk in hope. Rejoice in Christ.

Reflection Questions

•Meditate on this: How often do you live in light of, and indeed center your daily life on, your justification in Christ?

_____

_____

•In the context of your day-to-day walk with the Christ, what does it mean to "stand in grace"?

_____

_____

•In what ways could you practically cultivate hope amidst your hardships?

_____

_____

Abba, Father, thank You for Your grace and mercy this morning, for loving me the way You do and that You are totally faithful and trustworthy. Father, forgive me for being so quick to join in judging others. Give me instead Your eyes to see those around me today who are thirsty. And give me Your heart to reach out to them where they are, to see them as You created them and to offer them respect, acceptance, love and the source of living water. In Jesus. Amen.

John 4:5-42 (NIV)

⁵So he came to a town in Samaria called Sychar, near the plot of ground Jacob had given to his son Joseph. ⁶Jacob's well was there, and Jesus, tired as he was from the journey, sat down by the well. It was about noon.

⁷When a Samaritan woman came to draw water, Jesus said to her, "Will you give me a drink?" ⁸(His disciples had gone into the town to buy food.)

⁹The Samaritan woman said to him, "You are a Jew and I am a Samaritan woman. How can you ask me for a drink?" (For Jews do not associate with Samaritans.)

¹⁰Jesus answered her, "If you knew the gift of God and who it is that asks you for a drink, you would have asked him and he would have given you living water."

¹¹"Sir," the woman said, "you have nothing to draw with and the well is deep. Where can you get this living water? ¹²Are you greater than our father Jacob, who gave us the well and drank from it himself, as did also his sons and his livestock?"

¹³Jesus answered, "Everyone who drinks this water will be thirsty again, ¹⁴but whoever drinks the water I give them will never thirst. Indeed, the water I give them will become in them a spring of water welling up to eternal life."

¹⁵The woman said to him, "Sir, give me this water so that I won't get thirsty and have to keep coming here to draw water."

¹⁶He told her, "Go, call your husband and come back."

¹⁷"I have no husband," she replied.

Jesus said to her, "You are right when you say you have no husband. [18]The fact is, you have had five husbands, and the man you now have is not your husband. What you have just said is quite true."

[19]"Sir," the woman said, "I can see that you are a prophet. [20]Our ancestors worshiped on this mountain, but you Jews claim that the place where we must worship is in Jerusalem."

[21]"Woman," Jesus replied, "believe me, a time is coming when you will worship the Father neither on this mountain nor in Jerusalem. [22]You Samaritans worship what you do not know; we worship what we do know, for salvation is from the Jews. [23]Yet a time is coming and has now come when the true worshipers will worship the Father in the Spirit and in truth, for they are the kind of worshipers the Father seeks. [24]God is spirit, and his worshipers must worship in the Spirit and in truth."

[25]The woman said, "I know that Messiah" (called Christ) "is coming. When he comes, he will explain everything to us."

[26]Then Jesus declared, "I, the one speaking to you—I am he."

[27]Just then his disciples returned and were surprised to find him talking with a woman. But no one asked, "What do you want?" or "Why are you talking with her?"

[28]Then, leaving her water jar, the woman went back to the town and said to the people, [29]"Come, see a man who told me everything I ever did. Could this be the Messiah?" [30]They came out of the town and made their way toward him.

[31]Meanwhile his disciples urged him, "Rabbi, eat something."

[32]But he said to them, "I have food to eat that you know nothing about."

[33]Then his disciples said to each other, "Could someone have brought him food?"

[34]"My food," said Jesus, "is to do the will of him who sent me and to finish his work. [35]Don't you have a saying, 'It's still four months until harvest'? I tell you, open your eyes and look at the fields! They are ripe for harvest. [36]Even now the one who reaps draws a wage and harvests a crop for eternal life, so that the sower and the reaper may be glad together. [37]Thus the saying 'One sows and another reaps' is true. [38]I sent you to reap what

you have not worked for. Others have done the hard work, and you have reaped the benefits of their labor."

[39]Many of the Samaritans from that town believed in him because of the woman's testimony, "He told me everything I ever did." [40]So when the Samaritans came to him, they urged him to stay with them, and he stayed two days. [41]And because of his words many more became believers.

[42]They said to the woman, "We no longer believe just because of what you said; now we have heard for ourselves, and we know that this man really is the Savior of the world."

Devotion

Have you ever been thirsty? Really thirsty? Truth is we all have...thirsty for love and acceptance...a place to belong...to know we matter...that our life has meaning and purpose.

The woman at the well was no different. It's a human thing, hardwired in all of us by God Himself, and only He can fill it. Problem is, like the woman at the well, we look in all the wrong places to quench our thirst. She had been through five husbands and still hadn't found that she was looking for.

So what did Jesus do? Rather than keep His distance from those rejected or judged most by society and the church in that day, He met them where they were and offered them the very thing they had been looking for in all the wrong places. He extended them respect, human dignity and the answer to the void they longed to fill. Living water—that deep, satisfying, intimate, faithful relationship with our Creator that restores meaning and purpose to our lives.

Brian Fikkert, in his book, *When Helping Hurts*, suggests the reason we reach out to others is to be an extension of Jesus Christ reconciling the whole world (God, self, others and creation) to Himself, all the while seeing ourselves as mutually broken and in need of each other to get there.

At Christ Church, our mission is to love Jesus and love like Jesus in the world. It's not complicated—keep it simple! Let's love like Jesus.

Reflection Questions

•Who are the Samaritans in today's world, those often judged rather than offered living water?

_____

_____

_____

• Who will God place in my path today who is thirsty?

_____

_____

_____

_____

• Will I remain distant or meet them where they are and offer them the only thing that will ever satisfy that deep longing in all of us?

_____

_____

_____

_____

_____

_____

Jesus, thanks for willingly laying down your life for me so that I can have eternal life. Help me to live a life worthy of Your sacrifice on my behalf. Amen.

Hebrews 10:4-10 (NIV)

> [4]It is impossible for the blood of bulls and goats to take away sins. [5]Therefore, when Christ came into the world, he said:
> "Sacrifice and offering you did not desire,
>   but a body you prepared for me;
> [6]with burnt offerings and sin offerings
>   you were not pleased.
> [7]Then I said, 'Here I am—it is written about me in the scroll—
>   I have come to do your will, my God.'"
> [8]First he said, "Sacrifices and offerings, burnt offerings and sin offerings you did not desire, nor were you pleased with them"—though they were offered in accordance with the law. [9]Then he said, "Here I am, I have come to do your will." He sets aside the first to establish the second. [10]And by that will, we have been made holy through the sacrifice of the body of Jesus Christ once for all.

Devotion

My wife and I are blessed to have three wonderful children—one son and two daughters. As parents, we join a host of you who have spent countless hours and dollars raising your children. Seven weeks ago we dropped our son off at Wake Forest to begin his college career. While my son rejoices and enjoys this new freedom and life experience, my wife and I are feeling new pain and suffering. The tears, the tuition check with all the zeroes and the sadness of our son living several hundred miles from home remind us of the willing sacrifice we parents make to provide life to our kids.

Hebrews 10:4-10 reveals to us that in a similar way Jesus willingly sacrificed His life for us. Christ's sacrifice contained many more zeroes than my tuition check and brings us greater hope than a degree will bring my children, but the parallels speak to our heart. Verses 4 and 8 tell us that the Old Testament sacrifices and offerings did not provide the complete and ultimate payment for the sins of the Israelites (or for us). Thankfully, verse 10 tells us that Christ's sacrifice made us holy, cleansing us, making us acceptable in our Father's eyes and providing us life in Him. Christ willingly laid down His life so that we might have the opportunity to be reconciled to God our Father through the ultimate, permanent, perfect sacrifice of Christ.

As you begin or end your day, consider the sacrifice you have made as a parent or that your parent made for you. Now, consider the value of Christ's willing sacrifice that brought you eternal life. While you had no way to obtain this on your own, Christ recognized your need and came to save you. As Paul writes in the scriptures, the proper response to this loving act is to live a life worthy of the Gospel of Christ.

Reflection Question

•In what way can you willingly lay down your life today in a manner worthy of Christ's sacrifice for you?

_____

_____

_____

_____

_____

SUNDAY

SHANE STANFORD

MARK 9:14-29

Just prior to this encounter, Jesus had returned from the mountainside with three of His disciples. While on the mountain, they had experienced nothing short of the magnificent glory of God, in what we call the Transfiguration of Jesus. Scholars have debated the significance of this event, many summarizing it as a mix between divine showmanship and the beginning of Jesus' march to the cross. Regardless, Jesus left the mountain with His eyes fixed on the mission ahead.

Peter, on the other hand, was so impressed that he planned to build three altars (one for each of the figures seen on the mountain) so that he could remember in worship what had taken place. The mountain meant something to those who witnessed the scene unfold. They didn't want "the moment" to end.

Nevertheless, Jesus encouraged His three disciples to assimilate what they had seen. He knew that no matter the glory of what they had experienced on the mountain, their work was not there. The solitude of the mountain is never the setting for what matters most in this world. The real work happens in the valley. No, our mountaintop time with God prepares us to meet the needs that are farthest removed from the quiet of our devotional lives.

So it is that upon returning to the valley, Jesus encounters a crowd in the midst of a difficult discussion with the religious leaders about healing. Jesus, whom they had thought was still away on the mountain, finds an excited, welcome response when the people realize He is among them.

It is here that Jesus first meets the father with the demon-possessed son. The father had brought his son to the disciples for healing, but the disciples were unsuccessful. Frustration had then led the father to the scribes and religious teachers, who seized on the situation as a way of casting doubt not only on the disciples' abilities, but on those of their Master as well. What an amazing scene! Here are Jesus and three disciples, who have just experienced one of the most important displays of divine power recorded in Scripture, surrounded by a desperate father with his sick son, the rest of the (seemingly powerless) disciples, the plotting religious leaders and a questioning crowd.

It reminds me of returning from a spiritual life retreat or really great church conference only to have others steal my joy with the "cares of this world." I wonder if Jesus rolled His eyes or rubbed his forehead, wondering, *Why did I come back again?* His frustration at the situation is evident and unmistakable: "You faithless generation! How long am I to put up with you?" (see Mark 9:19, RSV).

Jesus is obviously frustrated with the continued lack of understanding from those around Him—and for the first time in scripture, we see Jesus openly question whether or not those whom He has chosen can actually follow Him. As Jesus stands amid the doubts of the scribes, the confusion of the disciples and the despair of the father, it seems clear to me that He can't help but think how far the mountaintop feels from this place. There, the powerful hand of the Father had been unveiled, but standing here in the midst of such confusion, considering both this situation and the future ahead, those mountaintop moments of transcendence seem like such a fragile glory.

Jesus clearly feels the frustration and loneliness that invade us all when we experience the presence of God and then come down from the mountain. As Jesus turns to address the concerns of the waiting father, we can't help but notice that Jesus has His own concerns and that His distress, whether or not it fits neatly into our theologies, tells us more about Christ than several mountaintops put together.

What frustrated Jesus when He returned from the mountaintop was not that the disciples couldn't heal the boy; it was that they couldn't grasp why they couldn't heal him. His disappointment is echoed each time we experience disillusionment with circumstances or relationships. Yet His response demonstrates how God steps in to remedy the situation: knowing our condition, understanding our struggle, seeing our imperfections and providing a way to progress. He doesn't just understand our struggle; He has felt it firsthand. God, in the Incarnation, made our fight His fight to the very core of His being.

As Jesus confronts the situation with the crowd, His first reaction is very human. He feels the need to make people "understand." He grows frustrated over the religious leaders' taunting and arguments, and the disciples' lack of faith saddens Him. Jesus wants to do *everything*. *Everything* is a source of great anxiety in our world. We believe that we must say yes to everything, that we must be all things to everyone and that we must provide answers for every question. No demand could be more pressing in our society, or more unattainable. Jesus feels this human desire raising its head, and He does what we all do: He grows frustrated. He tells them, "Bring the boy to me" (Mark 9:19). And so, the father brings the boy before Jesus.

Let me ask you a few questions: Where do you start when facing the struggles of this world? Where do you begin when confronted with frustration? How do you cope with imperfection in and around you? How do you live faithfully today when tomorrow is so uncertain and looks so bleak?

How do we begin any significant journey? *One step at a time.* How do we love the whole world? *One person at a time.* How do we confront the uncertainties of tomorrow? *One hope at a time.* Because taking on tomorrow's problems today will always lead to despair. Yes, He knows our shortcomings, for He was willingly bound by the same limitations. He doesn't expect us to do everything. But can't we start with *something*?

As the father of the demon-possessed son brings his son before Jesus, his faith is nearly gone. When Jesus asks how long the affliction had held the boy in its grasp, the father responds,

"Since childhood" (Mark 9:21). Then he adds, "If you can do anything, take pity on us, and help us" (Mark 9:22).

When we first read this statement by the father, most of us replay *"If you can . . ."* over and over. *Doesn't this man know who Jesus is?* Of course he does. But he is not just another person seeking Jesus' help. No, he approaches Jesus as the father of a sick child. He wants to believe, but it's not his fate that hangs in the balance. The possibility that he might not be able to take care of his son scares him. How can he trust someone else to do what he cannot?
"If I can?" Jesus replies. "Don't you know that all things are possible for those who believe?" (see Mark 9:23).

The father of the sick child responds immediately: "I do believe; help me overcome my unbelief" (Mark 9:24).

For years, I did not understand the paradox of this answer. How can one believe and yet *not* believe at the same time? It seemed a contradiction until I became a father. Now, however, it is clear to me that the father believes as well as anyone else could in that situation—after all, he is here asking for help, right? He knows Jesus' reputation and understands the power of His ministry. But in this moment, he also knows that in the deepest places of his heart, he fears that Jesus cannot do what He says He can do. There is just enough distance between the belief in his mind and the belief in his heart to create a place where doubts linger and anxiety rises. The father's fear betrays his lack of trust. The emotional and physical strain of the son's illness has caused the father to lose not his faith, but his *assurance* in faith. As a man, he believes in God; as a father, he struggles to trust. His doubt is not spiritual rebellion. On the contrary, the burden for his child outweighs the grasp of the faith he so dearly wants.

The father of the sick child pleads that Jesus might not only heal his son, but—greater still— heal his own doubt. In that moment of unbelief, he thinks, *I am his father. No matter my doubts, I must believe that there is an answer. Jesus must do the rest.*

Jesus rebuked the demons, and they left the child. He walked over and took the boy by the hand, lifting him from the ground. And then, scripture states clearly, the child stood up under his own strength (see v. 27).

I wonder what was going on in Jesus' mind as He helped the child stand. Was He still frustrated at the scoffing of the religious leaders and the confusion of the disciples? I think not. No, in touching the child, Jesus reminded the onlookers and maybe even Himself what the Good News promises. In an encounter filled with failure, doubt and frustration, a standing boy brings the message back to center stage and reminds those watching why Jesus' ministry means so much to so many.

As the action moves inside the house, the disciples ask Jesus why they couldn't heal the boy. After all, the disciples had healed and performed miracles such as this before (see Mark 3). What was different this time? Jesus responds, "This kind [of demon] can come out only by prayer" (v. 29). I don't believe He is talking here only about the demon within the boy. No, "this kind" is any force that keeps a person or group of people from seeing and doing the work of God before them. Such demons come in many forms. Could it be the demon of doubt plaguing our thoughts, the demon of frustration veiling our joy, or the demon of anger preventing us from seeing the Messiah in our midst?

By "prayer," Jesus is referring to the disciples' relationship with God. The deeper our prayer life, the closer we are to Him. Quite simply, Jesus tells the disciples that they couldn't rid the child of his demon because they had moved away from God. In essence, they had rearranged their spiritual proximity and that had made all the difference. Why? Because even though they had been given the gift once, there was no guarantee that it would continue unless they remained close to the Father.

Jesus wasn't condemning the disciples—He was reminding them that the power of God works only if the conduit is open. As in every other aspect of our relationship with God, He does not force His will upon us. No, there comes a point that, even if after feeling His touch once, we must choose to receive and respond again. Remember that, in the end, even the boy must choose to stand up with Jesus.

Do you remember the Sunday school picture of Jesus standing at the door, knocking? A friend of mine provides a new take on this much beloved scene. He insists that Jesus is not asking if He can come inside as much as He is asking us *to come outside with Him*.

Friend, it's time to get rid of your demon, whatever that may be, and stand up with God. Trust me, God is more than aware of your doubt and frustration; He knows the deepest and darkest places of your soul. He knew the doubts harbored by the father of the sick child and, time and again, we see a glimpse of Christ's own struggles.

Satan wants you to believe that any feeling of uncertainty is wrong or somehow blasphemous. What a lie! Remember, Satan's best tool is not to overtly attack our lives. No, his greatest weapon is when he convinces us that we can't be honest with God—no matter that God already knows the core of our self-deception. Unfortunately, many times, we would rather believe the lie than face the weakest link—our greatest fear.

What incredible courage the father had in admitting that he didn't know how to shed his doubt and unbelief. After all, no one could have been more in need or have had a greater desire to give the *right* answer than he. But what did the father do? He didn't just give the right answer; he chose to give the *honest* answer: "I do believe, help me overcome my unbelief!" (see Mark 9:24). Most of us in a similar situation would tell Jesus what we think He wants to hear, or at least the "most spiritual" thing we could think to say. Yet this father spoke from his heart. He had nothing to prove and everything to lose . . . his son.

Jesus did what the father asked because God doesn't play games with us. He knows how complicated and bewildering this mixed-up world can be. Remember the focus of this encounter: Jesus knows the limitations of our lives and understands the foundations of our fears firsthand.

Knowing this, friend, take heart—your doubts and fears are not enough to make God turn away. Christ walked the journey too and was burdened by the same imperfections of this world.

This encounter comforts me because I realize that God knew very well the feelings of that father. God, too, had everything to lose—His Son—but He chose to do just that for you and for me. He did so because God knows the other side of our limitations—the potential in us that we cannot see—and His Son ensures that our imperfections don't define us in the end.

Reflection Questions

What is your greatest fear?

_____

_____

If you are a parent, like the father in this encounter, what about the thought of helplessly watching as your sick child fights for life? His story touches the fragile, vulnerable places of human existence. Jesus met a father who wanted to believe, but because of circumstances, didn't know how. This passage is about limitations—the boy's struggle with the demon, the father's struggle with unbelief and the disciples' struggle to heal them both. God understands our limitations and desires that we not remain bound by them.

Why does Jesus' frustration both teach and comfort us as to how much God loves and accepts us?

_____

_____

_____

_____

The Bible says to "wait patiently for the Lord"(Psalm 27:14a). But that is very difficult, especially in hard times. Life's limitations create three kinds of unbelief—those who *can't* believe; those who *won't* believe; and those who *want* to believe, but don't know how. Which one are you? Why?

_____

_____

Make a list of things for which God can't forgive you. It's a short list, right? If God's love knows no limits, then neither must our limits define how we connect to God.

_____

_____

_____

_____

Why is it important for us to live faithfully as the Body of Christ in the world? What difference does it make to be the "hands and feet" of Jesus to the most vulnerable among us?

_____

_____

_____

_____

_____

_____

Lord, we know Your greatness was foretold; You allow us to share in this excitement and redeeming grace that only You can provide. Prepare our hearts and our minds to understand and accept the beauty of Your earthly life so we may one day bask in Your heavenly glory. Father, take our lives and transform them into directional guides that point others to Your love and sacrifice for us. Help us to remember in any circumstance that nothing is impossible with You. Thank You, Father, for Your never-ending love; it is in Your name we pray. Amen.

Luke 1:26-38 (NIV)

[26]In the sixth month of Elizabeth's pregnancy, God sent the angel Gabriel to Nazareth, a town in Galilee, [27]to a virgin pledged to be married to a man named Joseph, a descendant of David. The virgin's name was Mary. [28]The angel went to her and said, "Greetings, you who are highly favored! The Lord is with you."

[29]Mary was greatly troubled at his words and wondered what kind of greeting this might be. [30]But the angel said to her, "Do not be afraid, Mary; you have found favor with God. [31]You will conceive and give birth to a son, and you are to call him Jesus. [32]He will be great and will be called the Son of the Most High. The Lord God will give him the throne of his father David, [33]and he will reign over Jacob's descendants forever; his kingdom will never end."

[34]"How will this be," Mary asked the angel, "since I am a virgin?"

[35]The angel answered, "The Holy Spirit will come on you, and the power of the Most High will overshadow you. So the holy one to be born will be called the Son of God. [36]Even Elizabeth your relative is going to have a child in her old age, and she who was said to be unable to conceive is in her sixth month. [37]For no word from God will ever fail."

[38]"I am the Lord's servant," Mary answered. "May your word to me be fulfilled." Then the angel left her.

Devotion

I remember the night my wife drove to my place of work in 2003 to tell me we were going to have our first child, Patrick. The event occurred 10 years ago; however, I never cease to get excited when I think of a new life entering the world and the potential impact that child will have. The excitement and fear of being a parent is only natural, and preparing for the coming of this new child took many twists and turns. I didn't know what to think or even how to act. Will my son be a ball player? Will my son find the cure for an obscure disease? Will my son be a businessman? There are so many unknowns regarding my son and what legacy he might leave if any. As I reflected on Luke 1:26-38, these were the thoughts that resurfaced instantly in my mind. I started to contrast the message I received with all the unknowns and uncertainty versus the message Mary received with all the confirmation and affirmation of our great Savior to come.

Luke recorded several details of the Christ child's birth as well as the dialogue His mother Mary had with the angel Gabriel. The word "will" in my story framed questions or unknowns. On the contrary, the word "will" or "shall" in Mary's encounter was prophetic, stating whom this child would be, from His name to His mission. Mary did not have to question who her son was to become because she knew who His heavenly Father was and is. We need to focus during this Lenten season, not on the unknowns of our lives, but the truth of who Christ is and His desire for our lives. The certainty we receive in this truth is one that WILL have kingdom impact for generations to come, and we know this because nothing is impossible with God.

Reflection Questions

•How do you think Mary felt when she heard she would have a child, the holy Son of God?

_____

_____

_____

_____

•Think about a time when you were excited about something that had not happened yet, like a vacation or a gift. Did it turn out exactly like you planned? Is God's love for us ever questionable?

_____

_____

_____

•What are some ways we can let others know about the awesome sacrifice Christ made for us?

_____

_____

_____

_____

•God has a purpose for our lives. Write down three ways you can be an example of God's love in your community, and try to live these out in the coming weeks. Write down what you think will happen and what actually happens when you live it out.

_____

_____

_____

_____

Gracious God, We begin today by looking to Your Word for a greater understanding of how you see the world. We pray that You will help us to recognize Your love, see Your hope in new places, feel Your desire for our life and witness Your vision in what we see in the world today. May You be glorified this day. Amen.

Samuel 16:1-13 (RSV)

¹The Lord said to Samuel, "How long will you grieve over Saul, seeing I have rejected him from being king over Israel? Fill your horn with oil, and go; I will send you to Jesse the Bethlehemite, for I have provided for myself a king among his sons." ²And Samuel said, "How can I go? If Saul hears it, he will kill me." And the Lord said, "Take a heifer with you, and say, 'I have come to sacrifice to the Lord.' ³And invite Jesse to the sacrifice, and I will show you what you shall do; and you shall anoint for me him whom I name to you." ⁴Samuel did what the Lord commanded, and came to Bethlehem. The elders of the city came to meet him trembling, and said, "Do you come peaceably?" ⁵And he said, "Peaceably; I have come to sacrifice to the Lord; consecrate yourselves, and come with me to the sacrifice." And he consecrated Jesse and his sons, and invited them to the sacrifice.

⁶When they came, he looked on Eliab and thought, "Surely the Lord's anointed is before him." ⁷But the Lord said to Samuel, "Do not look on his appearance or on the height of his stature, because I have rejected him; for the Lord sees not as man sees; man looks on the outward appearance, but the Lord looks on the heart." ⁸Then Jesse called Abinadab, and made him pass before Samuel. And he said, "Neither has the Lord chosen this one." ⁹Then Jesse made Shammah pass by. And he said, "Neither has the Lord chosen this one." ¹⁰And Jesse made seven of his sons pass before Samuel. And Samuel said to Jesse, "The Lord has not chosen these." ¹¹And Samuel said to Jesse, "Are all your sons here?" And he said, "There remains yet the youngest, but behold, he is keeping the sheep." And Samuel said to Jesse, "Send and fetch him; for we will not sit down till he comes here." ¹²And he sent, and brought him in. Now he was ruddy, and had beautiful eyes, and was handsome. And the Lord said, "Arise, anoint him; for this is he." ¹³Then Samuel took the horn of oil, and anointed him in the midst of his brothers; and the Spirit of the Lord came mightily upon David from that day forward. And Samuel rose up, and went to Ramah.

Devotion

Our scripture passage reveals how David was first anointed as King. David's coronation did not come with the pomp and circumstance that we are used to seeing in the world today. Instead, it was a humble affair. Unaware, David had to be called in from tending to his flock. How did this happen?

Samuel was mourning over Israel's first king—Saul. The Lord appears and tells Samuel that the time has come to stop grieving because the Lord has chosen a new king. The Lord has to almost force Samuel to get on with the anointing. But instead of disciplining Samuel for not immediately attending to the task at hand, the Lord comforts him by addressing all his concerns and leading him step-by-step.

Samuel arrives in Bethlehem and invites the elders and the family of Jesse to participate in a sacrifice. When everyone is present, the sons of Jesse walk in front of Samuel. Seeing the oldest son, Samuel reacts by assuming that he must surely be the one the Lord has chosen. After all, he is a good-looking man, he is the oldest and, therefore, he must be the "proper" one to select. The Lord quickly tells Samuel that appearance carries no weight with Him.

The next son comes, and he is not chosen either. Five more sons are led in front of Samuel all with the same result. But wait, there is one more son. The least of the sons in terms of stature (he was ruddy) and the last in the rank of this family. He had not even been worthy of being included in the sacrifice with Samuel. They had to run out and get him from the field. Yet this shepherd from a less than powerful family was the one the Lord had chosen.

How encouraging that the Lord does not see as we see! Imagine if we took the time to see people as the Lord sees them—by seeing the heart and not the outward appearance. Beyond that the Lord breaks our conventional thinking by using people in *new* ways that are for His purposes. God works in and through all things even when we cannot see how it could work.

Do you also see how similar David's beginning was to Jesus? Jesus was from a small little town with nothing good to offer (John 1:46). Joseph and Mary could only afford the minimum offering of two doves after his birth (Luke 2:22-24). David was a shepherd who would be king. Jesus is a King, and He became a shepherd for us.

Reflection Questions

•What is something that you first looked and judged to be worth very little that turned out to be immensely valuable?

_____

_____

_____

_____

•God has a plan even when we cannot see it or understand it (Isaiah 55:8). Are you following the Lord's call even if you cannot clearly perceive His plan? Or are you sitting still making excuses about why you cannot move?

_____

_____

_____

_____

•Are you limiting God's ability to work in a situation that you cannot see your way past (Isaiah 59:1)?

_____

_____

_____

_____

Lord Shepherd, as we go through today, no matter where we find ourselves, may we see that You are all we need. May You become our want. Amen.

Psalm 23 (RSV)

¹The Lord is my shepherd, I shall not want;
²   he makes me lie down in green pastures.
He leads me beside still waters;
³   he restores my soul.
He leads me in paths of righteousness
   for his name's sake.
⁴Even though I walk through the valley of the shadow of death,
   I fear no evil;
for thou art with me;
   thy rod and thy staff,
   they comfort me.
⁵Thou preparest a table before me
   in the presence of my enemies;
thou anointest my head with oil,
   my cup overflows.
⁶Surely goodness and mercy shall follow me
   all the days of my life;
and I shall dwell in the house of the Lord
   forever.

Devotion

I love this psalm. It is one of the most beloved pieces of scripture in church history. It's probably one of the most recognized in the world. This psalm is just so comforting. No matter where I find myself, I know the Good Shepherd will provide. Comfort is defined.

As I take a closer look, there is a challenge in this psalm. What makes the psalmist so comforted? Is it the waters or the pasture? Is it the rod and staff in darkest places? Is it the banquet table? Is it the blessing of the anointing and the cup? Look at the verbs the psalmist gave those things: restores, comfort and overflows. It would certainly seem that way, but I'm not so sure.

I think the answer is in the first verse. "The Lord is my shepherd, I shall not want." That is the whole psalm. The rest of the psalm is a description of the beginning. David understands that he has everything in the Good Shepherd. David understands the Good Shepherd is not just the source of the blessings, He is the blessings. He's not a cosmic middle man, a means to an end. The Lord is the means and the end. He is the provider and the provision. David has found contentment in the Lord.

This understanding David has is powerful. Now he sees goodness and mercy everywhere he goes, in any situation or circumstance. The Good Shepherd is the green pasture, the still waters, the rod and staff, the banquet table, the anointing and the cup. The Lord is the goodness and the mercy that follow him.

The same is true in the end as the beginning. David finds himself in the house of the Lord. He began with Him and finished with Him because they were together all along.

Remember, as you go, you too have a Good Shepherd. He is more than a companion on the path. He is the Path. He is the Provider and the Provision. He is the Way, the Truth and the Life.

Reflection Questions

•In what ways is God revealing Himself as the Good Shepherd in your life?

_____

_____

_____

•What is a concrete way God has shone His provision for you?

_____

_____

_____

•In what ways has worshipping with the church reaffirmed God's love for you?

_____

_____

Loving God, during this season of Lent, deepen our desire to live as children of light. Through Your eyes give us vision, so that we may perceive Your light in dark places and find Your grace even in the midst of suffering and death. Forgive us when we fall short, so that we are enabled to rise with Christ each day. May Your light shine through us for all to see. In the strong name of Jesus we pray, Amen.

Ephesians 5:8-14 (NIV)

[8]For you were once darkness, but now you are light in the Lord. Live as children of light [9](for the fruit of the light consists in all goodness, righteousness and truth) [10]and find out what pleases the Lord. [11]Have nothing to do with the fruitless deeds of darkness, but rather expose them. [12]It is shameful even to mention what the disobedient do in secret. [13]But everything exposed by the light becomes visible—and everything that is illuminated becomes a light. [14]This is why it is said:

"Wake up, sleeper, rise from the dead, and Christ will shine on you."

Devotion

As I cradled our new granddaughter in my arms, I was filled with unspeakable joy. Her tiny face radiated with a beautiful innocence that awakened within me the assurance of the presence of God's love. In the moment, I experienced a ray of hope breaking into my heart not only for this special child, but also for all creation. Intuitively, I kissed her cheeks and forehead and then softly spoke her name, *Phoebe*, in her ear. Phoebe…a name chosen by her parents that Mark and I had rarely heard. We knew no one called by that name. Yet, Phoebe already seemed to fit this child well.

Our daughter Claire, the baby's mother, reminded us that Phoebe was a deacon of the church at Cenchreae who gave great support and help to Paul and others (see Romans 16:1-2). Although there is no concrete evidence, many biblical historians believe that Phoebe may have been the person who Paul entrusted with the responsibility of delivering his letter to the church in Rome. In Greek, Phoebe means "bright shining light."

As I continued to gaze into Phoebe's bright, alert face, I found myself praying that she too will be one who has Jesus as the star in her life. Perhaps she is a kind of living example of what Paul meant when he wrote to the Ephesians advising them to follow Jesus as "children of light." My thoughts drifted toward how much darkness and evil our Phoebe and billions of other little children are destined to face in this troubled world. Nevertheless, hope radiates from Christ, the Promised Child, just as it does from the innocent face of every newborn baby.

Paul deftly connects our call *to walk in the light* as a metaphor for overcoming evil. He knows that such a walk means the elimination of wrongdoing not only within and among ourselves, but also in the whole culture around us. As Christians, we face the awesome task, not only of avoiding evil, but also of exposing it to the light as well.

In part, this means engaging in a relentless search for the light of truth. Several years ago on a trip highlighting the second and third missionary journeys of Paul, our group toured the ruins of Ancient Ephesus. From the location and magnitude of the remaining façade of the library, we were struck by the importance placed on acquiring knowledge. The Apostle Paul must have visited the library and marveled at the volume of enlightenment it wrought. Could he have known what his own writings would come to produce—the light diminishing the world's darkness through authentic Christian witness?

We are called to be participants in more than a search for truth, more than a quest for holiness and personal piety. The risen Christ beckons us to be bearers of His light every day. Paul and Phoebe and martyrs and saints before us inspire us to be "the light of the world."

Reflection Questions

•Where is the Spirit calling/empowering you to be Christ's light in the world today?

_____

_____

•What evil in our society do you most feel needs exposure and uprooting right now?

_____

_____

_____

•What other scriptures reinforce or expand your understanding of the "light of Christ"?

_____

_____

Great God of mercy and healing, come pass us by and open our eyes. Open them to see Your glory and the commands You have set before us. Give us the courage to follow those commands, even in face of great adversity. Even when it seems that we are walking through the valley of the shadow of death, let us remember that it is You who gave us sight, and it is You who guides us. Amen.

John 9:1-41 (NIV)

¹As he went along, he saw a man blind from birth. ²His disciples asked him, "Rabbi, who sinned,this man or his parents, that he was born blind?"

³"Neither this man nor his parents sinned," said Jesus, "but this happened so that the works of God might be displayed in him. ⁴As long as it is day, we must do the works of him who sent me. Night is coming, when no one can work. ⁵While I am in the world, I am the light of the world."

⁶After saying this, he spit on the ground, made some mud with the saliva, and put it on the man's eyes. ⁷"Go," he told him, "wash in the Pool of Siloam" (this word means "Sent"). So the man went and washed, and came home seeing.

⁸His neighbors and those who had formerly seen him begging asked, "Isn't this the same man who used to sit and beg?" ⁹Some claimed that he was.

Others said, "No, he only looks like him."

But he himself insisted, "I am the man."

¹⁰"How then were your eyes opened?" they asked.

¹¹He replied, "The man they call Jesus made some mud and put it on my eyes. He told me to go to Siloam and wash. So I went and washed, and then I could see."

¹²"Where is this man?" they asked him.

"I don't know," he said.

¹³They brought to the Pharisees the man who had been blind. ¹⁴Now the day on which Jesus had made the mud and opened the man's eyes was a Sabbath. ¹⁵Therefore the Pharisees also asked him how he had received his sight. "He put mud on my eyes," the man replied, "and I washed, and now I see."

¹⁶Some of the Pharisees said, "This man is not from God, for he does not keep the Sabbath."

But others asked, "How can a sinner perform such signs?" So they were divided.

¹⁷Then they turned again to the blind man, "What have you to say about him? It was your eyes he opened."

The man replied, "He is a prophet."

¹⁸They still did not believe that he had been blind and had received his

sight until they sent for the man's parents. ¹⁹"Is this your son?" they asked. "Is this the one you say was born blind? How is it that now he can see?"

²⁰"We know he is our son," the parents answered, "and we know he was born blind. ²¹But how he can see now, or who opened his eyes, we don't know. Ask him. He is of age; he will speak for himself." ²²His parents said this because they were afraid of the Jewish leaders, who already had decided that anyone who acknowledged that Jesus was the Messiah would be put out of the synagogue. ²³That was why his parents said, "He is of age; ask him."

²⁴A second time they summoned the man who had been blind. "Give glory to God by telling the truth," they said. "We know this man is a sinner." ²⁵He replied, "Whether he is a sinner or not, I don't know. One thing I do know. I was blind but now I see!"

²⁶Then they asked him, "What did he do to you? How did he open your eyes?"

²⁷He answered, "I have told you already and you did not listen. Why do you want to hear it again? Do you want to become his disciples too?"

²⁸Then they hurled insults at him and said, "You are this fellow's disciple! We are disciples of Moses! ²⁹We know that God spoke to Moses, but as for this fellow, we don't even know where he comes from."

³⁰The man answered, "Now that is remarkable! You don't know where he comes from, yet he opened my eyes. ³¹We know that God does not listen to sinners. He listens to the godly person who does his will. ³²Nobody has ever heard of opening the eyes of a man born blind. ³³If this man were not from God, he could do nothing."

³⁴To this they replied, "You were steeped in sin at birth; how dare you lecture us!" And they threw him out.

³⁵Jesus heard that they had thrown him out, and when he found him, he said, "Do you believe in the Son of Man?"

³⁶"Who is he, sir?" the man asked. "Tell me so that I may believe in him." ³⁷Jesus said, "You have now seen him; in fact, he is the one speaking with you."

³⁸Then the man said, "Lord, I believe," and he worshiped him.

³⁹Jesus said, "For judgment I have come into this world, so that the blind will see and those who see will become blind."

⁴⁰Some Pharisees who were with him heard him say this and asked, "What? Are we blind too?"

⁴¹Jesus said, "If you were blind, you would not be guilty of sin; but now that you claim you can see, your guilt remains."

Devotion

What a story this is! Here we have a man who has been blind since his birth, who knows absolutely nothing of the gift of sight, and finds himself blessed enough to be in the path of Jesus as He passes by. Jesus, in a way that is totally unique to

Himself, spits on the ground, mixes the spit with the dirt to make clay, and then rubs the clay on the man's eyes. The man at this point must be thinking, "This is not at all what I had in mind… and it's kind of gross." Then Jesus tells the man to "Go, wash in the Pool of Siloam" (John 9:7, NIV), and I'm sure he's thinking, "Great, because this is gross." He obeys Jesus' command, and he is healed.

However, instead of an eruption of joy among the people, this man is almost immediately called to defend himself against those who question the validity of his previous blindness as well as the validity of Jesus Himself—who is now, all of a sudden, nowhere to be found.

The Pharisees try to do everything they can to get this man to deny Jesus. They even try and turn his own parents against him. They say to him, "Give God the praise; we know that this man is a sinner." But he understands what Jesus has done for him. He may not fully understand how Jesus did it, or why, but the one thing he is absolutely certain of is "that though I was blind, now I see."

We who are in Christ oftentimes find ourselves in the same boat. We have decided to give our lives to God, to obey His command, and sometimes that is met with resistance. We may have a hard time understanding all of the pushback because, after all, we are doing what God has called us to do, so why should it be as hard as it seems?

These are questions that we will not always have the answers to. It may be hard to trust that God knows exactly what He is doing. But in all that, take heart; for one thing is absolutely certain, once we were blind, and through the great love and mercy of Christ, we now see! And just like the man in the end of this story, one day we will stand face-to-face with our glorious Savior. We will see Him for all of His wonder and beauty, and we will be able to respond in worship!

Reflection Questions

•What are the things God has called you to do in this season of your life?

_____

_____

•What are some things in the past month that have been discouraging to you as you try to be faithful to God's call on your life?

_____

_____

Sunday

SHANE STANFORD

JOHN 8:1-11

Several readings into the first verses of John 8, it occurred to me that the woman brought before Jesus literally landed at His feet. We often move quickly to the rest of this story—the woman's actions and what she was accused of—without taking notice of the scene itself. Here is Jesus kneeling, or sitting maybe, in the Temple square while this woman, probably not looking her best, is thrown or pushed by angry men to the ground at His feet. The place is dusty, hot and dirty. Others gather around just in time to hear those who have brought the woman to Jesus declare her crime—adultery—and the punishment—death.

Push the pause button and hold this image in your mind. This is important. You have the angry accusers, the woman and Jesus. Oh yes, and you have those who have gathered, though even they can't really tell you why. That is the nature of angry mobs. We gather because the action intrigues and distracts us. But who are we kidding? We also gather because something deeply broken inside of us likes it—unless you are the woman on her knees, her face in the dirt at the feet of Jesus.

And that is the missing part of the story—the woman, how she felt and what had brought her to this place. Read from her point of view, this is a painful passage. Her hopelessness is as obvious as the dirt on her face, and there appears to be little that Jesus can do. She is caught in a riptide and is barely holding on. This is nothing short of a rescue mission—there is no other way to describe it. Maybe that is the reason so many of us have read this passage half-heartedly, focusing on the woman's sin or the "gotcha" encounter between Jesus and the religious leaders. These are important, yes, but there is much more here—too much for us, perhaps. The woman's helplessness feels familiar, and as we watch her story unfold, we realize that this is a story about us, about the neighbors we have known and about the many times we have forgotten one another in order to save ourselves.

Who is to blame? And the same question always seems to be the first in my mind when I read about the woman caught in adultery. It is easy to blame her. She doesn't have much of a defense; she has been caught in the act and she doesn't deny the charges. No, the only thing that saves her is Jesus, whose few wise, quick-witted words make the woman's accusers feel guilty enough to walk away. Any other woman in any other square with any other teacher but Jesus, and things would have turned out very differently.

But back to the question: Is the woman the only one to blame in this story? I'm not much of an expert on adultery, but I know enough to realize that adultery doesn't happen alone. For every adulterer, there is a willing accomplice. Yet the woman is the only one dragged to the street. Was one of her accusers also a customer? Who knows?

I get the feeling that Jesus knew the woman's predicament. Sure, she's not exactly living a noble life, but what has driven her here? It's almost certain that she had not chosen this path. Was it her only option? Scripture doesn't say, yet history reminds us that women in Jesus' day were grossly undervalued, and those who couldn't find a suitable husband and family often resorted to other means for making a living. For every bad decision, there is a series of bad decisions, made by more than one person, leading up to it. This woman's sin was not her choice alone. No, it took place within a relationship, alongside the choices of her accomplice. But, as happens so many times in situations like this, she is alone, abandoned, when she lands in the dust at Jesus' feet. I imagine that Jesus more than knows the depth of her sin, but He also knows that her abandonment issues, rooted in the bad decisions of others, are part of the problem.

Let me say again for those of you needing to cling to this point: The woman was guilty. She had committed sins against herself and grievances against the faith. The Law prescribed death for such a trespass. But where the letter of the Law stops, Jesus begins. One lesson Jesus teaches throughout His ministry is that sin does not happen in a vacuum; we are interconnected to the core of our lives. Jesus' confrontation with the woman's accusers opens the door for a new kind of spiritual conversation, one rarely heard in the legalistic religion they practiced.

No one in the crowd understands the Law better than Jesus. In fact, He understands not only the Law but also the way the woman's accusers are trying to use it to trap Him. The Law in its most elementary form attempts to confront sin and eradicate its impact. Read within the context of the Jewish faith and culture, there is nothing wrong with the purpose of the Law. Truth is never the problem, right? If you have ever had to confront adultery face to face, you understand how painful and destructive it is. It affects not only the individuals involved; it has a dramatic impact on an entire community. Who wouldn't want to drive adultery from our midst?

But this encounter isn't just about adultery, at least not the kind committed between two individuals. This is about human nature, and I am not talking about sexuality or desire. No, I mean something even more dangerous: the twistedness of human nature that divides us from our brothers and sisters by convincing us that our condemning thoughts, feelings and actions can be justified for personal survival. Let me ask you, *What is the worst kind of adultery?* The act committed by two people caught in a sexual relationship, or the adultery committed against God when we believe that we can pronounce His judgment on our brothers and sisters? In doing so, do we not make ourselves our own god? And, in doing that, do we not replace God with someone else? Isn't that cheating on God? Isn't that the definition of adultery? I believe Jesus would say yes.

As the scene develops, Jesus begins to write in the dirt. What is this all about? Is He biding His time? Is it a rabbinic trick? Or does Jesus' action symbolize what He knows—that the dirty details of the woman's sin can't hold a candle to the filth encrusting the hearts of those around her?

It's worth noting that Jesus answers the accusers' questions, but never disagrees with the part of the Law they so dearly want Him to recognize. In fact, He confirms its seriousness and then takes it one step further: "If any one of you is without sin, let him be the first to throw a stone at her" (John 8:7). His reply stops the self-righteous leaders in their tracks. Scripture describes them dropping their stones one by one, beginning with the oldest, as though the more mature among them understands what Jesus is doing: With one sentence, He affirms the Law and reminds everyone of its intended purpose. Man, I like this guy!

You see, friend, Jesus understood that the woman was not the only person in need of a new start. She wasn't the only one suffering from a sickness that doctors couldn't heal. The woman was not the only lost and forgotten soul who needed to see the light that the Good News announced. No, Jesus understood that the woman's story was the story of every person surrounding her that day, and the story of each of us today. The grace of Christ doesn't just reach for those lying in the dirt; it reaches for those of us who choose to stand in judgment. Jesus knew the woman, but He knew her accomplice and He knew the accusers, too.

I believe God grows weary of our need to hurt and condemn one another in such quick fashion, especially given the state of our own souls. He knows that we all need to be freed from the bondage of our sinful choices and the bad decisions of others.

Let me give you an example. My wife and I have an amazing marriage . . . now. It has not always been so. For several years while I pastored a new church, our marriage nearly unraveled. One day we awoke to realize that we were held hostage by mistakes and misguided intentions. Although we had not committed the same sin as the woman, Pokey and I both found ourselves lying in the dirt at the feet of Jesus. Ironically, we stood in judgment, too—stones in hand, ready to pummel one another. In fact, as we looked closer at the story of the woman caught in adultery, we discovered a bit of ourselves in every character. It was unnerving. But we also realized some powerful truths about our marriage and about our faith. Taking the time to assess our dusty conditions and wonder if we really were prepared to throw those stones made us see how much more we wanted, how much more we needed in God. It was a difficult time, but confronting it together in the love of Christ changed our marriage forever.

Let me be clear: God does not like sin. God does not like adultery. God does not like the pain we cause each other. But God also doesn't like us to decide what each other's fate will be. No, that decision belongs to God; He alone makes that call.

And if Jesus' encounter with the woman caught in adultery is any indication, that is reason for hope.

"Where have your accusers gone?" Jesus asks her. In doing so, He clears the path of her sin, her rejection, her loneliness, her pain and her past, so that she can see and take hold of a new and better way. The first step to freedom in Christ, whether we're lying in the dirt or hefting a rock in our hand—or both—is to turn away from the past toward the future God intends for us.

There are worse things than dying; sometimes, living is much harder. The woman in the dirt at Jesus' feet understood this. She experienced spiritual attacks brought on by the Adversary whose intention was to break her heart. Though the circumstances may be different, many of us experienced attacks meant for the same purpose. The assault may come from an illness, from a bad relationship, from past mistakes, but regardless what form they take, the goal is to so drain our lives of hope that we find ourselves lying in the dirt, wishing the end would come. Some of us, covered in the grime of shame and tasting the grit of regret, even figure it would be easier to die than to live like this.

But Satan doesn't want to kill you—he wants to own you at the lowest bargain price he can negotiate. His trouble is, he can't close the deal alone; he needs your signature on the contract. The woman caught in adultery came close to making the sale. She had convinced herself there was no hope, that she had gone too far for anyone to care. What followed? Self-doubt, self- loathing, self-destruction . . . and hopelessness. Why change? Why bother? The woman, in her feelings, expectations and actions, had become her own worst enemy.

But don't just blame her; she had help. And I'm not just talking about her accomplice in adultery. The entire crowd played a part. How ready they were to stone her! How many of them could have made a difference in the woman's life but turned away instead? Maybe they so feared revealing their own failings that they needed to punish her—partly for her transgressions, sure, but mostly for their own.

Too easily, Satan convinces us to believe the lies we tell ourselves and each other. We don't need the whole story, just enough of the lie to plant a seed of doubt. One seed planted here and another one there, until they have grown into a full-blown patch of weeds, choking every corner of our lives. The weeds take root and become a fixture in our relationships, our thought patterns and our spiritual walk. Finally, after a while, it is difficult to remember what led us here, much less how in the world we escape from such a place.

The way out of these lonely, desperate places is not as difficult as it seems. The Adversary needs us to believe that turning the tide is too risky, that it takes too much effort and is too costly. The truth? It only takes one moment to turn things around. The woman caught in adultery found her moment in the dirt. As one stone after another dropped to the ground, Jesus posed this question: "Woman, where are [your accusers]? Has no one condemned you?" (John 8:10).

When she looked up, she saw that the crowd had gone. "No one condemns me," she uttered (see John 8:11).

"Then neither do I condemn you," Jesus declared (John 8:11).

In that moment, the woman's future changed. She had become accustomed to rejection. She had understood the sneers and stares. She had expected the gossip and hateful whispers. But she had not been prepared for Jesus. He had given her the benefit of the doubt, and it was likely the first time anyone had ever offered her such a gift.

And what an amazing gift it was! To live your entire life with everyone expecting the worst only to find, at the darkest hour, Someone who believes in you. You can't buy it, earn it, trade your body for it. No, it is what it is: an offering of grace that changes the way you view life and its possibilities. It's true that this gift doesn't change the circumstances or details immediately, but it gives you a new starting point, and you can't help but believe that there must be a better way than the one you have traveled.

The world sometimes succeeds in convincing us that certain things are inevitable and that certain patterns created in our lives cannot be changed. *Once trouble, always trouble.* But do you really think God believes it? I don't—too much evidence indicates otherwise. The Gospel narrative points again and again in stories like this to God's hope for us, long before we have hope for Him. Jesus' love for you and me, shown in every one of His teachings and interactions, points to the high value God places on each of our lives and the potential He sees in each of us. If we are valuable enough for Jesus to become like us, will He not offer each of us the chance to turn from the past, brush off the dirt and become more like Him?

John 3:16-17 still tells the story of God's intentions for every person lying prone in the dirt of their lives. Let me paraphrase: *God loved us so much that Jesus came to be like us, so that everyone who believes in Him will find real life, now and forever. Oh . . . and if this is the case, then certainly God didn't send Jesus to condemn but to restore us.* This is the heart of the Gospel, the hope for the world.

We condemn—ourselves, each other, even God—because it is easier than believing what God has given to us in Christ. Christ's plan is not to condemn. God knows the ease of condemnation— pass judgment, wipe your hands, a day's work done. Instead, Jesus' words to the woman set out the primary principles to guide us in our relationship with God and with others. *I choose not to pass judgment because I am offering a second chance, so that not only will you see the potential of a life restored, but others will, too.* In those few words, Christ offers forgiveness, a challenge and a new beginning.

And critics on both sides are left speechless. Those who rush to judgment find in Jesus a new standard of grace and forgiveness. Those who claim that His "love for sinners" is measured by cheap faith with no accountability find that God expects us to do better. Jesus' forgiveness and restoration of the woman send a signal to everyone: *Sin is serious business in which each person here is employed, and now I'm making it My business.* The scene of the woman landing in the dirt at Jesus' feet is personal and uncomfortable because we can't help but see ourselves in one character or another . . . and, like it or not, we're in this together.

In his wonderful book *The Ragamuffin Gospel,* Brennan Manning writes: "After long hours of prayer and meditation on the Scriptures and reflection on the nagging question 'Who Am I?' a gracious God has given me the light to see myself as

I really am. I now have a primary identity and a coherent sense of myself. It affects my intimacy with God, my relationships with others, and my gentleness with myself."

If you, like Brennan and like the woman caught in adultery, feel as if you are living in the dirt, I have a question for you: Would you like another chance, maybe a new start? Then stop throwing stones at yourself, and stop repeating the same choices that land you at Jesus' feet time and again. You were meant for more than this. Christ knows it; you should, too. Don't sell your soul at a bargain price. Lift your head and look around. Where are your accusers? God believes in second chances. Do you?

If, on the other hand, you are standing in the crowd—as an accuser or just a curious bystander—let me tell you this: Many of our brothers and sisters feel God's absence because we help them to believe it by our rejection, sneers, gossip or indifference. People believe the lies when no one bothers to tell them the truth. Will you really be the first to throw a stone?

Whether we are lying in the dirt or practicing our aim, Jesus asks, *Wouldn't you rather stop the game? Here is one of your own in trouble—if she can't play, shouldn't we all sit this one out?*

This encounter places each of us in the picture. We see the best and worst of ourselves, and it is time to decide who we will be in this world. The crowd has gathered around, the accusers are waiting. The dirt is hot and dusty. But this is not a game, and the stones will do damage. My sister, lying in the dirt—and my brother, the stone in your hand— what will it be?

Reflection Questions

Many of us believe that we know this story, but do we? As the woman landed at Jesus' feet, the scene collides with our hearts and minds, unfolding from many angles. Jesus seemed to know the road that led her to His feet and the condemnation that had so defined her; He knew the woman. But He also understood that adultery doesn't happen alone. Make no mistake: As the woman lay abandoned in the dirt, Jesus knew her accomplice. Finally, Jesus knew that the woman's accusers had all, in their own way, committed adultery against God. And isn't that the case with us all? Stoning another person means not having to focus on our own sins. Jesus saw the inner workings of the human heart. We cannot leave this scene without a keen sense of God's seriousness about the problem of sin in each of us as well as the power of forgiveness for all of us.

Sin is a sickness from which all of us suffer. Why is the darkness in our lives so difficult to recognize and oftentimes so hard to confront?

_____

_____

What keeps you "landing at Jesus' feet" in need of forgiveness? Who accuses you today? Or are you another character in the story? Are you the accuser of another brother or sister? Are you the accomplice?

_____

_____

_____

_____

_____

_____

Why do we rush to judgment when perceiving others? How does our sin in not accepting others with the grace of Christ continue the cycle of sin and brokenness?

_____

_____

_____

The Bible says that "nothing can separate us from the love of God" (Rom. 8:38). God's grace heals our hearts and then moves us forward. Jesus says to go and sin no more. Is that possible? Why or why not? What might "sinning no more" look like? What keeps that picture from becoming reality in your life?

_____

_____

_____

WEEK 6 | DAY 1 | MONDAY
Ezekiel 37:1-14 | Josh Smith

Father, breathe new life into this passage by Your Spirit, that we might see the point at which the depth of Your Deity intersects the brokenness of our humanity and offers redemption to all who would live, even Christ Himself, the Lord of Life. Amen.

Ezekiel 37:1-14 (NIV)

[1]The hand of the Lord was on me, and he brought me out by the Spirit of the Lord and set me in the middle of a valley; it was full of bones. [2]He led me back and forth among them, and I saw a great many bones on the floor of the valley, bones that were very dry. [3]He asked me, "Son of man, can these bones live?"

I said, "Sovereign Lord, you alone know."

[4]Then he said to me, "Prophesy to these bones and say to them, 'Dry bones, hear the word of the Lord! [5]This is what the Sovereign Lord says to these bones: I will make breath[a] enter you, and you will come to life. [6]I will attach tendons to you and make flesh come upon you and cover you with skin; I will put breath in you, and you will come to life. Then you will know that I am the Lord.'"

[7]So I prophesied as I was commanded. And as I was prophesying, there was a noise, a rattling sound, and the bones came together, bone to bone. [8]I looked, and tendons and flesh appeared on them and skin covered them, but there was no breath in them.

[9]Then he said to me, "Prophesy to the breath; prophesy, son of man, and say to it, 'This is what the Sovereign Lord says: Come, breath, from the four winds and breathe into these slain, that they may live.'" [10]So I prophesied as he commanded me, and breath entered them; they came to life and stood up on their feet—a vast army.

[11]Then he said to me: "Son of man, these bones are the people of Israel. They say, 'Our bones are dried up and our hope is gone; we are cut off.' [12]Therefore prophesy and say to them: 'This is what the Sovereign Lord says: My people, I am going to open your graves and bring you up from them; I will bring you back to the land of Israel. [13]Then you, my people, will know that I am the Lord, when I open your graves and bring you up from them. [14]I will put my Spirit in you and you will live, and I will settle you in your own land. Then you will know that I the Lord have spoken, and I have done it, declares the Lord.'"

Devotion

One of my favorite songs is "Bones of You" by the British band Elbow. The lyrics poignantly capture the melancholic grief that can overwhelm our memories of sweeter times. In this case, it's the Gershwin classic "Summertime" that reminds our poet of a love lost "five years ago and three thousand miles away." Some experiences have a way of transporting us to moments of reminiscence so devastatingly vivid that the tension and distance between the glorious "then" and the bitter "now" seem simply unbearable.

Perhaps this was the case for Ezekiel as he surveyed the bones of an army long since stripped of life. As far as he knew, oblivion was the final word for these men who were to be a symbolic picture of the now disgraced and exiled Israel. What a terrible tension Ezekiel must have felt, balancing his memory of former glory of God's people with this tragic wasteland of humanity. "Can these bones live again?" Maybe Ezekiel's response was akin to that of Samwise Gamgee from *The Lord of the Rings*, who asked Gandalf with hopeful incredulity if everything sad would come untrue. It was the question the disciples dared not ask when the very Son of God had been torn from the land of the living—an irreversible injury in the minds of those whom He had left behind. Perhaps it's a question you've asked yourself about your vocation or marriage or your youthful ambitions, maybe even your currently ailing body. Life restored? "Only You know, Lord."

And then everything changed. Here in this passage we see a hope that had not yet in scripture been so luridly revealed—that of the Glorious Resurrection. By the breath of the Living God, dust can and shall return to life. And nothing is so final a word as the Resurrection of Christ, whose death was no less tragic a loss than all others combined. This was not to be the end of the story. Scripture testifies with conclusive clarity: those stories that end badly for the people of God are always either untrue or simply unfinished. The words of the Lord to Ezekiel must have echoed in the minds of the disciples that day: "And then you shall know that I am the Lord." Indeed, He is the Lord of Life, the Lord of the Harvest, First Fruits of the Resurrection from the Dead and Redeemer of all that was once lost.

Reflection Questions

• Do you think Ezekiel had any hope for Israel prior to this prophetic encounter with God?

_____

_____

_____

_____

_____

_____

• In what ways does bodily resurrection stand against an abstract view of a disembodied afterlife?

_____

_____

_____

_____

•How does the hope of the Resurrection shape your view of loss in this life?

_____

_____

_____

_____

Lord, I am desperate for You today. I confess that I am drowning in sin and disobedience and that You are my only hope of salvation. Thank You for Your promises of forgiveness and redemption through Jesus that give breath to my soul. I will wait expectantly for You to show me more of who You are that I may know You better and love You more. Amen.

Psalm 130 (NIV) *A song of ascents*

> [1]Out of the depths I cry to you, Lord;
> [2]Lord, hear my voice.
>
>   Let your ears be attentive
> to my cry for mercy.
> [3]If you, Lord, kept a record of sins,
>   Lord, who could stand?
> [4]But with you there is forgiveness,
>
>   so that we can, with reverence, serve you.
> [5]I wait for the Lord, my whole being waits,
>
>   and in his word I put my hope.
> [6]I wait for the Lord
>
>   more than watchmen wait for the morning,
>
>   more than watchmen wait for the morning.
> [7]Israel, put your hope in the Lord,
>   for with the Lord is unfailing love
>
>   and with him is full redemption.
> [8]He himself will redeem Israel
>   from all their sins.

Devotion

This anonymous psalm begins with a cry of anguish and pleading for the Lord to listen and show mercy. "Out of the depths" refers to the depths of the ocean and brings to mind a person in danger of drowning, crying out for help and rescue. What particular event or circumstance has brought the psalmist to this place of desperation and brokenness is not known, but the feeling is familiar to us all. Sometimes, it is through no fault of our own that we are struggling, while other times, it is because of our choices that we are barely able to keep our heads above water.

Our world is reluctant to name that thing that weighs us down and causes us to feel as though we are drowning. Our postmodern society reasons that if we say there are no absolute truths—no right or wrong— we will be free of guilt and shame. But we, as followers of Christ, know that this is absolutely untrue! Our sin is the lead weight that pulls us under the raging seas, leaving us exhausted and unable to take the hand of God as He reaches out to rescue us through forgiveness. We cannot fully understand the love and mercy God has shown us in Christ without recognizing and repenting of the sin in our lives. The assurance that God keeps no record of sins after confession and forgiveness gives us true freedom from shame, guilt and condemnation.

The tone of the psalm changes with the word "But." You can almost hear the drowning man draw in his first unlabored breath after being rescued! Forgiveness changes everything, and it is found in God alone. As the forgiven, we must forgive so that we may honor and serve God.

There are two ways we can wait for the Lord. The first is to wait passively, wishing and hoping for the best possible outcome. The second way is to wait expectantly, putting our hope in God and His Word, as the psalmist describes. A watchman would wait for morning, not wishing and hoping it would come, but knowing, without a doubt, it would come. We can wait on the Lord with the same assured expectation knowing that He will keep all of His promises.

The psalmist gives encouragement to the people of God to put their hope in God, who does not disappoint. His unfailing love and the promise of the redemption of their sins were extravagantly expressed in the person of Jesus, who came to rescue drowning sinners like you and me.

Reflection Questions

•When you feel like you are drowning, to whom do you cry out?

_____

_____

_____

_____

•How do you handle waiting on the Lord?

_____

_____

_____

_____

•How does your life reflect the unfailing love, grace and mercy that have been shown to you by God?

_____

_____

_____

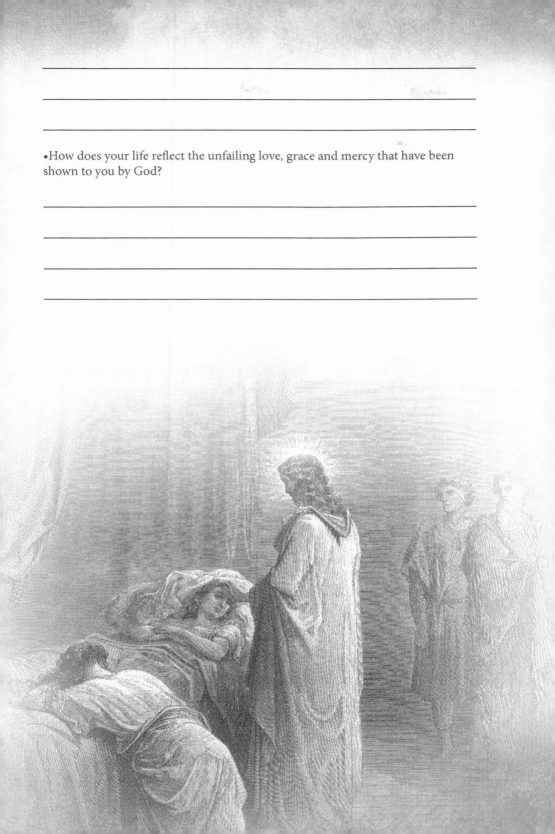

Father, help be to believe the Gospel today: that I am made new from the inside out and have everything I need for life and godliness in Christ. My tendency will be to not believe this and thus act like the former me—seeking for things of this world to scratch the itch of my fleshly desires. But in Christ and by the Spirit, it is possible to not only believe differently but also live differently. Help me to think upon and live out of that truth today. Amen.

Romans 8:6-11 (NIV)

⁶The mind governed by the flesh is death, but the mind governed by the Spirit is life and peace. ⁷The mind governed by the flesh is hostile to God; it does not submit to God's law, nor can it do so. ⁸Those who are in the realm of the flesh cannot please God.
⁹You, however, are not in the realm of the flesh but are in the realm of the Spirit, if indeed the Spirit of God lives in you. And if anyone does not have the Spirit of Christ, they do not belong to Christ. ¹⁰But if Christ is in you, then even though your body is subject to death because of sin, the Spirit gives life because of righteousness. ¹¹And if the Spirit of him who raised Jesus from the dead is living in you, he who raised Christ from the dead will also give life to your mortal bodies because of his Spirit who lives in you.

Devotion
You could say I had waited my whole life for this moment. I was a senior in high school playing on the baseball team. We had made it to the state championship final, and it was my turn to pitch. It was an average year for me, to say the least, and my coach had lost a lot of confidence in my abilities to pitch well enough to win the "big game." I had even begun to doubt myself and started believing that I wasn't good enough and that the coach was perhaps right. But something rose up in me that day, and I decided to defy the odds of what I felt. For some reason, the voice in my heart telling me "I could do this" became louder than the voice of others that questioned *if* I could do this. I walked up to the coach, told him I was going to pitch and how I would win us this game. The rest is history. I pitched the best game of my life, and we won the championship.

I think a lot of us feel the same when it comes to following Jesus. We get so focused on the things of this world and our ravenous desires that we forget to simply set our mind on the Spirit. What does this mean? It means that when I think I am not loved or respected enough at my work, from my spouse, or my friends, I can choose to run to and fill myself up on the things of this world that only *seem* to give me what I'm looking to find, or I can listen to the Holy Spirit remind me of the good news: that I have everything I need for life and godliness in Christ. This means I have all the love and respect I will ever need because of what Christ has accomplished for me on the cross and through His Resurrection. What a wonderful truth to hold to; what a wonderful reality the Holy Spirit is always trying to remind you and me of and convince us to believe.

Sure, the flesh makes a lot of noise and gets the best of us many times. But what would it look like to let the melody of grace spoken by the Spirit become louder than the noise of this world spoken by the flesh? It simply takes us being willing and open to say, "Holy Spirit, speak the Gospel to my heart and remind me of who I am in Christ once more today."

Reflection Questions

• What are the situations of life that draw my attention away from believing the good news of Christ in my life?

_____

_____

_____

_____

• Do I actually believe that the Holy Spirit is trying to speak to me and remind me of the good news of Christ in my life?

_____

_____

_____

_____

• If so, how could I make space to set my mind on the melody of the Spirit today (that I have everything I need in Christ) instead of the noise of the flesh (that I don't have everything I need in Christ and need to go and find it through my flesh instead)?

_____

_____

_____

Gracious Father, we ask You to strengthen our faith, increase our love and renew our desire to serve You. May we reflect on Your immeasurable sacrifice as we seek to love others as You have loved us and to walk in Your Resurrection power for Your glory. Amen.

John 11:1-45 (NIV)

¹Now a man named Lazarus was sick. He was from Bethany, the village of Mary and her sister Martha. ²(This Mary, whose brother Lazarus now lay sick, was the same one who poured perfume on the Lord and wiped his feet with her hair.) ³So the sisters sent word to Jesus, "Lord, the one you love is sick."

⁴When he heard this, Jesus said, "This sickness will not end in death. No, it is for God's glory so that God's Son may be glorified through it." ⁵Now Jesus loved Martha and her sister and Lazarus. ⁶So when he heard that Lazarus was sick, he stayed where he was two more days, ⁷and then he said to his disciples, "Let us go back to Judea."

⁸"But Rabbi," they said, "a short while ago the Jews there tried to stone you, and yet you are going back?"

⁹Jesus answered, "Are there not twelve hours of daylight? Anyone who walks in the daytime will not stumble, for they see by this world's light. ¹⁰It is when a person walks at night that they stumble, for they have no light."

¹¹After he had said this, he went on to tell them, "Our friend Lazarus has fallen asleep; but I am going there to wake him up."

¹²His disciples replied, "Lord, if he sleeps, he will get better." ¹³Jesus had been speaking of his death, but his disciples thought he meant natural sleep.

¹⁴So then he told them plainly, "Lazarus is dead, ¹⁵and for your sake I am glad I was not there, so that you may believe. But let us go to him."

¹⁶Then Thomas (also known as Didymus) said to the rest of the disciples, "Let us also go, that we may die with him."

¹⁷On his arrival, Jesus found that Lazarus had already been in the tomb for four days. ¹⁸Now Bethany was less than two miles from Jerusalem, ¹⁹and many Jews had come to Martha and Mary to comfort them in the loss of their brother. ²⁰When Martha heard that Jesus was coming, she went out to meet him, but Mary stayed at home.

²¹"Lord," Martha said to Jesus, "if you had been here, my brother would not have died. ²²But I know that even now God will give you whatever you ask."

²³Jesus said to her, "Your brother will rise again."

²⁴Martha answered, "I know he will rise again in the resurrection at the last day."

²⁵Jesus said to her, "I am the resurrection and the life. The one who believes in me will live, even though they die; ²⁶and whoever lives by believing in me will never die. Do you believe this?"

²⁷"Yes, Lord," she replied, "I believe that you are the Messiah, the Son of God, who is to come into the world."

²⁸After she had said this, she went back and called her sister Mary aside. "The Teacher is here," she said, "and is asking for you." ²⁹When Mary heard this, she got up quickly and went to him. ³⁰Now Jesus had not yet entered the village, but was still at the place where Martha had met him. ³¹When the Jews who had been with Mary in the house, comforting her, noticed how quickly she got up and went out, they followed her, supposing she was going to the tomb to mourn there.

³²When Mary reached the place where Jesus was and saw him, she fell at his feet and said, "Lord, if you had been here, my brother would not have died."

³³When Jesus saw her weeping, and the Jews who had come along with her also weeping, he was deeply moved in spirit and troubled. ³⁴"Where have you laid him?" he asked.

"Come and see, Lord," they replied.

³⁵Jesus wept.

³⁶Then the Jews said, "See how he loved him!"

³⁷But some of them said, "Could not he who opened the eyes of the blind man have kept this man from dying?"

³⁸Jesus, once more deeply moved, came to the tomb. It was a cave with a stone laid across the entrance. ³⁹"Take away the stone," he said.

"But, Lord," said Martha, the sister of the dead man, "by this time there is a bad odor, for he has been there four days."

⁴⁰Then Jesus said, "Did I not tell you that if you believe, you will see the glory of God?"

⁴¹So they took away the stone. Then Jesus looked up and said, "Father, I thank you that you have heard me. ⁴²I knew that you always hear me, but I said this for the benefit of the people standing here, that they may believe that you sent me."

⁴³When he had said this, Jesus called in a loud voice, "Lazarus, come out!" ⁴⁴The dead man came out, his hands and feet wrapped with strips of linen, and a cloth around his face.

Jesus said to them, "Take off the grave clothes and let him go."

⁴⁵Therefore many of the Jews who had come to visit Mary, and had seen what Jesus did, believed in him.

Devotion

Perhaps the first thing we notice in this passage is that Jesus allowed His friend Lazarus to die, in spite of His great love for him. But God loved Jesus and allowed Him to die, too. God always has a bigger plan, yet, sadly, we often challenge His plan instead of trusting the one who can even "raise the dead" (Hebrews 11:19).

Martha and Mary trust Jesus, in spite of their deep grief, such that when Jesus finally arrives in Bethany, Martha greets Him with faith, "I know that even now God will give you whatever you ask" (John 11:22). But her faith is tested when Jesus asks that the stone be taken away. Martha balks, "But Lord, by this time there is a bad odor" (John 11:39). *Surely you're not going to expose Lazarus in this embarrassing and unpleasant way!*

Like Martha, so often we trust God to do things *our* way, instead of His. Will you let go of this barrier to your faith? God wants to do great things through us that He will *not* do when we refuse to trust that *His* way is the best way.

Jesus had a plan to do more than just raise Lazarus from the dead. For one, He planned to strengthen the faith of those nearby. Jesus called them to remove Lazarus' filthy grave clothes, but would they do this uncomfortable deed to help their friend? Would they "get down and dirty" to obey the Son of God? Would they trust Jesus?

Is God calling *you* to do the uncomfortable? How would He have you administer His grace to someone in need? Perhaps filthy bonds of sin are smothering someone you know. Will you trust Jesus and lovingly come alongside to help free him or her for a new life in Christ Jesus?

Jesus' plan on this day was to glorify the Son of God and the Father (John 11:4). Truly, only God and the Son of God could raise a man from the dead, and through the raising of Lazarus, many would put their faith in Jesus. But others would seek to kill Him. The death and resurrection of Lazarus point to the glorious death and resurrection of Christ. Through these, God has redeemed us from sin and unified us to Himself. When we choose to live in that unity, with Christ *and* each other, God is most glorified.

Reflection Questions

•Are you struggling to love one, or some, of your Christian brothers and sisters? Remember, Jesus loved them enough to go to the cross.

_____

_____

•For God's glory, will you renew your goal to live in unity in the Body? Will you take steps today to love those you have failed to love?

_____

_____

O Lord, our Heavenly Father, who orders all things for our eternal good, mercifully enlighten our minds and give us a firm and abiding trust in Thy love and care. Silence our murmurings, quiet our fears and dispel our doubts that, rising above our afflictions and our anxieties, we may rest on Thee, the Rock of everlasting strength. Amen.

Psalm 118:1-2, 19-29 (NIV)

> [1]Give thanks to the Lord, for he is good;
> > his love endures forever.
> [2]Let Israel say:
> > "His love endures forever."
>
> [19]Open for me the gates of the righteous;
> > I will enter and give thanks to the Lord.
> [20]This is the gate of the Lord
> > through which the righteous may enter.
> [21]I will give you thanks, for you answered me;
> > you have become my salvation.
> [22]The stone the builders rejected
> > has become the cornerstone;
> [23]the Lord has done this,
> > and it is marvelous in our eyes.
> [24]The Lord has done it this very day;
> > let us rejoice today and be glad.
> [25]Lord, save us!
> > Lord, grant us success!
> [26]Blessed is he who comes in the name of the Lord.
> > From the house of the Lord we bless you.
> [27]The Lord is God,
> > and he has made his light shine on us.
> With boughs in hand, join in the festal procession
> > up to the horns of the altar.
> [28]You are my God, and I will praise you;
> > you are my God, and I will exalt you.
> [29]Give thanks to the Lord, for he is good;
> > his love endures forever.

Devotion

As the opening and closing verses of Psalm 118 might suggest, it is ordinarily categorized as a song of thanksgiving. "Give thanks to the Lord, for he is good; his love endures forever" (Psalm 118:1 & 29).

But Psalm 118 is also unique. It is the concluding psalm of the Hallel (Psalms 113-118), which came to be used at Passover.

But the early Christian community lay claim to Psalm 118 as well. They identified the speaker in verses 5-18, 28 as Jesus. According to the Gospels, when Jesus entered Jerusalem shortly before His crucifixion, He was greeted by a crowd in a manner reminiscent of Psalm 118.

In Mark 11:9, the first part of the greeting consists of Psalm 118:25a, 26a. "Blessed is he who comes in the name of the Lord." The use of Psalm 118 at this point is not really surprising since Jesus enters Jerusalem during the week of Passover.

But this observation does not exhaust the significance of Mark's use of Psalm 118. Verses 22-23 were understood within first-century Judaism to refer to the Messiah. "The stone the builders rejected has become the cornerstone; the Lord has done this, and it is marvelous in our eyes." Matthew 21:42 cites these same verses to suggest that Jesus is the rejected Messiah.

For all the Gospel writers, Psalm 118 is a means of understanding and articulating the significance of Jesus. In other words, by articulating the significance of Jesus through Psalm 118, the Gospel writers profess that the life, death and resurrection of Jesus have become in Christian liturgical tradition not just a psalm for Palm/Passion Sunday, which celebrates Jesus' entry into Jerusalem, but also for Easter as well.

For Christians, Easter is above all "the day on which the Lord has acted" (Psalm 118:24). "This is the day that the Lord has made; let us rejoice and be glad in it." God was active in the life, death and resurrection of Jesus. The Gospel writers affirm this in their use of Psalm 118.

But verse 24 is also a reminder to Christians that every Sunday is a celebration of the Resurrection, the Lord's Day, the day on which the Lord has acted and is still active. Thus, Psalm 118 can be seen as a focal point for discerning the continuity between the Old and the New Testament witnesses that God is for us (Psalm 118:6-7) and that "God's steadfast love endures forever" (Psalm 118:1-4, 29, ESV).

Reflection Questions

•What is the theme of Psalm 118?

_____

_____

_____

_____

•Who are the builders in verse 22? What "stone" do they reject? What is a cap-stone? (See Zechariah 4:7-9 & Acts 4:10-11.)

_____

_____

_____

_____

•In what ways had God been active in Psalm 118?

_____

_____

_____

_____

_____

Sunday

SHANE STANFORD

JOHN 11:1-44

When we read the Gospels, it is easy for us to think of Jesus walking and teaching around the Palestinian countryside as His band of disciples merrily follows behind. I call Him "Touring Jesus." In this version, the Twelve and Jesus travel from one venue to another, stopping long enough on the mountainside, along the shore or under a tree to dispense the word of wisdom for the day or to perform a miracle. But in reality, the Gospels present a very different picture of Jesus' ministry.

First of all, the travel conditions were wearying and cumbersome, and Jesus' ministry territory stretched from one end of Jewish Palestine to another, occasionally even crossing into Gentile territories. As a traveling preacher, Jesus would have experienced a lot of discomfort. Sure, He was God, but He was also fully human. I'm sure He smelled, felt and acted like any weary traveler. Not exactly the clean and shiny image we have of the Messiah.

Second, like any other traveler of His era, Jesus relied on the kindness of friends and supporters for the basic necessities. Scripture tells us that Jesus did not have a place to call His own (see Matthew 8:20; Luke 9:58), but instead counted on the hospitality of others to provide food, rest and relaxation (see Luke 10:38). Given the geography Jesus' ministry covered, it was convenient for Him to have certain places He stayed whenever He was in a particular area. The home of Mary, Martha and Lazarus in Bethany was one such place.

Third, because of His reliance on these stops and given the nomadic nature of Jesus' ministry back and forth across Palestine, He would have stopped frequently in these places. And, given such frequent visits, the relationships He developed with these particular followers would have been significant.

Scripture tells us that Jesus felt at home with Mary, Martha and Lazarus (see Luke 10:38-42; John 12:1-8). We can't be sure how and why they came to play such an important role in His ministry, but their support of and dedication to Jesus is unquestionable. Some accounts place Mary (possibly as a troubled young woman or even a person of ill repute) at the center of Jesus' connection to the family. Yet it's clear from the Gospels that Jesus loved not only Mary but also her sister and brother, and theirs was an enduring friendship.

But this was more than a personal relationship. The family supported Jesus' ministry and vocation, and they hosted, on at least one occasion, others who came to hear Jesus teach (see Luke 10:38-42). Their home was more than a stopover for His travels; it was a teaching center as well.

Jesus treated this family from Bethany as friends and considered them an important part of His ministry and life. It is clear that as much as they needed Jesus, Jesus also needed them, and He appreciated their care for Him and His disciples.

Jesus built enduring relationships that went beyond the roles of teacher and student. We can't picture Jesus only as the rabbi marching through Galilee spouting lessons for living. No, He built real relationships. Jesus had friends.

Think about that for a moment. It is an important concept that many modern believers miss.

If Jesus had friends, then He loved some folks more deeply than others (admit it . . . that idea makes you nervous!). I'm not referring to the grand, cosmic Love that God has for each one of us, Love that by its very nature cannot be more or less or play favorites; I'm talking about the love that any human has for another, especially if they have shared profound moments of success and struggle. It stands to reason that if Jesus was fully human, as the scriptures insist, and if He had people in His life who supported and cared for Him during His ministry, then He would have a deeper, personal connection to those folks.

I tried out this theory on several minister friends of mine recently, and they reacted like jealous girlfriends. I was completely unprepared for how they resisted the notion that Jesus could have loved some friends more than others. When I asked them why the idea bothered them so much, they responded with theological arguments, including the impeccably logical (and my personal favorite), "Well, He's Jesus."

When I went so far as to point out that in *our* ministries we are all guilty of having parishioners to whom we feel closer than others, one friend, who may be the smartest of all of us, froze spiritually (you could see it on his face) and was only able to utter, "But we are human."

"Well, wasn't Jesus supposed to be human like us?" I questioned.

"Yes, but . . ." he replied.

"But what?" I countered. "If Jesus was human, then wouldn't He have loved some people more than others? What are you so worried about?" I asked.

My friend stood silent for a moment and then answered, "I'm just not sure that I like Jesus being *that* human."

The conversation got me thinking: If Jesus was human enough to need resources and a place to sleep during His earthly ministry, that means Jesus needed people to provide assistance. And if Jesus needed people, then the ones who responded to His needs would naturally see a more intimate side of Him. And if they saw a more intimate side of a fully human Jesus, then would they not also experience the depth of His response for their care? And, at such depths of personal relationship, would not Jesus call them friend? I mean *real* friends. Not just a "friend of God" friend, but an "I've got your back" friend?

As you know, there is a difference, and that difference affects us in profound ways. "I've got your back" friendships shape who we are and form the heart of what matters in our lives. I don't believe it was any different for Jesus. Jesus needed people. He needed friends. I believe that Mary, Martha and Lazarus were these kinds of friends to Jesus, and I believe He needed them and loved them very much.

The first lesson of this encounter is that Jesus needed people. Jesus had friends.

Jesus teaches us that relationships are more than momentary connections; they mirror the very essence of who God created us to be. He not only talked about these connections, but He also lived them in His friendships with people like Mary, Martha and Lazarus. (And if such friendships are to mean anything in this world, they must also weather a hairline fracture or two in order to become invulnerable to change, disruption and even death. More about that in a minute.)

I have asked you this question before, but let me ask it again: *Why was it necessary for Jesus to walk among us in order to redeem us?*

Could it be that Jesus had to make friends and see imperfections and feel loss, just like us, in order to accomplish His mission? Jesus always goes to the heart of what we dread in this world. We dread being alone, so we make friends. We dread being hurt, so we don't make friends. We dread feeling betrayed, so we don't let our real selves show. We dread loss, so we choose not to love. If Jesus' friendships teach us nothing else, they remind us that He understands the intrinsic needs, wounds and fears of our lives.

Why all the talk about Jesus and friends and mushy stuff? What about the dead guy?

Right, Lazarus! We're getting to him.

If you read the Scripture passage prior to reading this chapter (if not, now is a good time!), you know that we have a dead guy (probably pretty content where he is), two very upset sisters and a bunch of confused bystanders, not the least of whom are the disciples. Jesus has tarried just long enough that Lazarus has not only died but has been dead for some while, leaving most Jews to believe that his soul had departed the body.

The religious leaders are mocking Jesus for not being everywhere at the same time (a precursor to the modern pastor-layperson relationship), and Thomas, God love him, is making proclamations about following Jesus to his death. (Thomas is an optimist.)

Where are you going with this? Let's get to the miracle already! Patience, my friend. Zero-ing in on the wrong thing is where most of us get into trouble.

When God seems to have vanished, when we feel completely alone, we have a tendency to believe one of two things. First, we believe that God and God's people *can't* love us. Or second, we believe that God and God's people *don't* love us. And when that happens, we retreat into some kind of junior-high self-preservation instinct that tells us we either need to run or fight because the situation has no solution.

Yet the earthly life of Christ, wrapped within the mysteries of what God was doing cosmically, points to some practical principles that God wants us to remember when the world is caving in on us. Jesus' ministry counters what the world would have us believe: *You must do it alone; you have to have a certain kind of smarts or be a certain kind of religious.*

For some reason, we tend to believe those voices in the back of our minds that say we have to be a certain way in order to have value or purpose. Of course, nothing could be further from what Jesus lives and teaches. Watch who He makes friends with and see how those friendships show what He values (the Beatitudes, for example, tell us a lot about the folks Jesus considered friends). The friends Jesus makes tell us more about Him and us and the whole world than any scripture, worship service or liturgy ever could. And when the going gets tough, Jesus' friendships remind us of a few indispensable notions that the Adversary would rather us forget—namely that humanity is wired for us to care for each other and do life together, because the Great Wirer, God, made us in His image. Relationships are why we are formed and how we experience, enjoy and survive the ups and downs of this place.

If such is the case, it's no surprise that relationships are the heart and soul of this encounter, which occurs because of great loss, the loss of a loved one. This loss leads several of Jesus' friends, previously unshakeable in their faith, to acutely feel God's absence. Truth be told, I don't believe this encounter and the subsequent miracle are just about Christ raising someone from the dead; in many ways, the miracle serves as the back story to the passage's real meaning. (Lazarus being raised from the dead may not even be in the top three reasons to take note of what happens here. Why? Because this is not primarily a lesson about being raised from the dead like Lazarus; it is more about living *like* Lazarus after he was raised.)

I believe the key verse in this passage is "Jesus wept" (John 11:35). But why did He weep? Did death affect Him that much? It would be naïve to think that Lazarus was the first person in Jesus' life who had died. Did He question whether or not He could raise Lazarus? Scripture tells us that He had already performed such a miracle for a Temple leader's daughter (see Mark 5:35-43) and a young man from Nain (see Luke 7:11-17). Did he fear the repercussions of a miracle such as this?

The Gospel of John hints that the resurrection of Lazarus catalyzed the plot to kill Jesus, but the other Gospels say that it was more a perceived threat to the authority of the

Pharisees from Jesus' rising popularity that sealed His fate. Given the other passages, raising someone from the dead alone didn't condemn Jesus. Yet if these were not the reasons, why did Jesus stand and weep at the grave of His friend? Further, the passage doesn't say He "teared up" or "felt misty eyed;" it says He wept. To understand what could bring such raw emotion from Jesus, we must go deeper, look inside the situation and seek to understand the real story happening in and around this tomb.

The key to understanding this encounter rests in watching Jesus confront the folks involved—the disciples (Thomas in particular), Mary and Martha, and, lest we forget, Lazarus—paying attention to their various reactions, and then watching Jesus respond. We will see that their reactions have less to do with Lazarus' death and everything to do with their own fears, beliefs and anxieties. I think you'll also see that our reactions in moments such as these say less about our grief than they do about our expectations of God in the midst of it.

Let's look at the disciples first. When the disciples heard that Lazarus was ill, they were already feeling overwhelmed by fear and anxiety. Jesus had angered the Establishment and He was now a marked man. The disciples didn't want to go back to Bethany, which was near Jerusalem and the religious leaders who had it in for Jesus, and they had (conveniently?) allowed Him to tarry for a couple of days before they set off. After all, the last time they were in Bethany, things didn't turn out well; the Jewish leaders had plotted to kill them. Jesus' returning to Bethany was, in the disciples' minds, not a wise move. If Jesus wanted to wait, fine with them; a "sleeping" friend didn't seem like a good excuse to risk life and limb.

It's not a stretch to say that the disciples downplayed Lazarus' need of Jesus. The word for "sleep" in Jesus' day had a dual meaning, and though the disciples were more than happy to interpret it as "slumber," given the context, they must have known there was more to it. Still, it was easier to convince themselves that Lazarus was napping than to face the danger of going back. Of course, some were obviously afraid for Jesus, but others of them were afraid for themselves.

While it's interesting that the disciples reacted to news of Lazarus' condition this way, it is not surprising. This is the tendency for many of us when things get uncomfortable or discouraging. The disciples retreated to a convenient excuse. When Jesus pushed the need to go further, their anxiety heightened. It is a story played out in our lives every day. Case in point: I have a friend who hates conflict. In fact, he will do whatever is necessary to avoid confrontation. Sometimes he allows himself to believe the most absurd excuses or explanation as a way of validating his unwillingness to resolve a dispute. In the end, the conflict only worsens and his anxiety increases. He eventually finds himself confronting the situation anyway, having only postponed the inevitable and made himself sick with worry in the meantime.

Jesus won't let the disciples get away with similar delay tactics. He wants to teach them a lesson about *time* and *courage*. He talks with them about "twelve hours in a day" (see John 11:9) because He wants the disciples to see the importance not just of time, but of *their* time, and He illustrates the proper, timely way to respond when God calls. It is easy to follow our natural instincts and retreat, allowing our fears and uncertainties to get the best of us—to spend time doing nothing but worrying. Yet what does God intend for how we use our time?

First, Jesus explains that God's time is perfectly set. Our work for God is never useless or in vain (see 1 Corinthians 15:58). Returning to Bethany is not only the right thing to do, bit it is also God's intention for them. Second, if God's timing is perfect, then they are equipped to respond with courage, trusting that God goes before them. Finally, as Jesus raises the temperature of the conversation, He implies that not only are they equipped to respond, they are *expected* to respond. Essentially, there is no more time to waste; one way or another, Jesus is headed toward Bethany, with or without the disciples.

Friends, we can't miss this point. God's plan often leads us into difficult situations. Regardless of the difficulty, God has made a way for us and we are expected to move forward. When we fail to respond to God's plan in our lives, we create a tension, not between God and us, but within ourselves. Most of us know when we have not done what is needed. We can excuse it or explain it away, but ultimately we must confront the truth of what it is: our predisposition to protect our selfish interests at the expense of God's work in our lives.

The reaction of the disciples shows us that when the forecast is bleak and danger is just over the horizon, some choose survival and run the other way.

In announcing that He would leave for Bethany, Jesus did what any friend would do. Yes, He had waited, but the passage never suggests that Jesus did not plan to go at all. Yet His delay gave rise to the question, in the minds of the disciples, of whether He would go or not. Listening to their debate, it might sound as if all of them felt the same way about Jesus returning to Bethany. That is, until Thomas spoke up.

Scripture portrays Thomas as passionate, emotional and skeptical. Most of us are familiar with Thomas' encounter following the Resurrection, when he asked to touch the scars of Jesus. He needed facts. His doubts were not about a lack of faith; on the contrary, Thomas' faith was great. No, his doubts were about getting enough information to ensure that he chose the right steps, no matter where they might lead. Regardless of our perception of him, Thomas was a responder; he just *qualified* his responses before making decisions. Thus, we shouldn't discount nor be surprised by Thomas' willingness and courage in following Jesus to Bethany. Not only was he prepared to go with Jesus, Thomas was prepared for whatever might come, including giving his own life. Thomas' courage is admirable; at least he took a stand for Jesus' decision. The disciples largely lacked courage; Thomas did not. No, Thomas lacked hope.

I have known many in my ministry who possess a strong sense of courage, but who have not experienced real hope. God wants both for us. A church member recently reminded me of the difference. During a Bible study meeting, I shared my experiences with heart surgery, and after the class that evening, a church member told me that she, too, had faced some difficult times in her life. As she weathered the storms and made her way through, she not only found courage to endure the event, she also realized that God intended for her to prevail in wonderful and unexpected ways.

She described in great detail how her life had fallen apart, affecting most of her relationships. Because of this stress, her physical health also failed, until finally she had lost almost everything. One night, however, while praying that God would either give her strength to survive or let her die (that's how bad the situation was), God audibly spoke to her. The words were from Jeremiah 29:11: " 'I know the plans I have for you,' declares the Lord, 'plans to prosper you and not to harm you, plans to give you hope and a future.'"

"It was in that moment," she said, "that I claimed the promise for my life that I didn't serve a God of *getting by* but a God of *going on to something better*." The language may seem flowery, but this particular church member did not use words lightly. She believed and lived as a person of hope.

I asked her if the situation had resolved itself as she wanted, and to my surprise, she said no. I stood back a minute, wondering where this was going, having assumed this would be a perfect story wrapped up in a bow and ready to be trotted out whenever I next needed an illustration about triumphing through struggle.

"It turned out better than I could have expected," she said. "What I had been praying was that God would give me the strength to endure. Instead, He gave me the hope to prevail." A beautiful expression crossed her face as she spoke those words. She was still amazed by what God had done. For a moment, I thought about how so often we forget to be amazed by the living God working in us.

"I don't want the details in one of your books," she said with a smile. "Just tell people that God has bigger plans for us than survival."

This conversation reminded me that God does not need us to join the "faith forces" and head into battle, although there are times when simple, grit-your-teeth courage is needed. No, God has better in store for us, and the better is abundance . . . now! We should not forget that even in the midst of our struggles, "in all things God works for the good of those who love him" (Romans 8:28).

Thomas reacted with great courage, and we should applaud that, but God has more in store for us.

When Jesus arrived in Bethany, He found a house full of mourners. This was not uncommon. In Jesus' day, when people died, family and friends were moved to action. Mourning was not sedentary; it involved a response both emotional and physical. Jesus would have encountered these mourners already gathered for long period of remembrance and ritual.

He would have also arrived to questions about why He was so late. Bethany was only a few miles away from where Jesus and the disciples had been, yet they did not arrive until the fourth day after Lazarus' death. I won't spend much time on the reaction of the crowd, because there is little evidence of what was actually said. But we all know human nature. As Jesus arrived, there would have been whispers about why such a close friend had not responded sooner. It's nothing new, and nothing has changed. There have always been and will always be those who, when the worst happens, presume to know what someone else's intentions really were and should have been. They are the Monday-morning quarterbacks of the Church who feel emboldened, almost compelled, to share an opinion or pronounce a verdict on a case about which they have no real knowledge. These folks are like flies at a picnic—maybe not enough to derail God's work, but annoying enough to disgust it.

Why is this important? Because no situation in our lives happens in a vacuum. Good or bad, our circumstances are affected by others—and vice versa. That is one of the results of being created to need one another and of being wired together in community. Community can spark the best of what God has created in us, but it can also unveil the worst.

This is where we find Martha, surrounded by friends and family, yet in the center of much anxiety and sorrow. Any of us who have faced the death of a loved one or friend knows the stress of these situations and the incredible sense of spiritual disruption that comes with it.

When Martha hears of Jesus' arrival, her reaction fits with her personality and provides a lesson for many of us like her. Martha is a person of action. Her brother is dead and she feels the need to solve the problem of her pain. She couldn't save him, but that doesn't alleviate her need to save *something*. Does this sound familiar? She needs to fix something, do something or make something, all in an effort to distract from the problem and numb the pain. Scripture does not detail it, but I can imagine the frenzy Martha is in as she goes through the obligatory mourning period.

Jesus' arriving is a relief to Martha, but it's also one more "responsibility" for her. Remember, she is a caretaker. Although Jesus, her friend, is here and could possibly provide answers to her many questions, Martha does not ask why this all has happened and, more importantly, why Jesus did not come sooner. Instead, Martha approaches Jesus as the good mourner/follower/ hostess. What she really wants to ask is "Why?" but Martha reacts to Jesus as many of us act with God. She really wants to ask, "Why weren't you . . . ?" "What happened?" "I thought you were a friend." But like Martha, rather than honestly asking the questions we need or want to know the answers to, we play nice: "I know if you had been here . . ."

Even after Jesus answers her with some of the most important words in all of the Gospel texts—"I am the resurrection and the life" (John 11:25)—Martha continues the pattern by giving an *academic* answer about resurrection. Again Martha is not honest about her feelings. Why? The answer lies in what I call "spiritual politeness disorder" (I just made that up, actually). I believe that, in most situations, we know very well what we are feeling; we just aren't willing to be honest with ourselves and with God. But how can we have real conversations about real issues in our lives and about our deepest emotions if we are unwilling to honestly approach God with our questions and disappointments? Martha's reaction is like some of the answers I have given when I have ministered to families in difficult situations who ask why God has allowed a particular event to happen. For instance, several years ago, a family in my congregation lost a young child to SIDS. It was one of the most difficult situations I have ever encountered. As I sat with the family, the father asked why this had happened. Feeling the need to respond in some way, and asking myself the same question, I gave a very academic answer, which boiled down to a defense of God and His sovereignty. The father looked at me politely but with little emotion. Thankfully, at that moment someone walked up and I was able to finish by asking the father if I could "get you anything."

Later, as we were leaving the home of the family, our church's minister of visitation, who was a retired layperson, said, "Can I ask you something?"

"Sure," I responded.

"Why didn't you just say you didn't know when the father asked why this happened?"

I paused, wanting to be honest with him. "I don't know," I finally answered, realizing how ironic it was that I was able to say the words now. "For some reason, I felt the need to explain God's actions."

"That's not your job . . . but you know that," he answered. "I know," I agreed.

"Your job is to be Jesus to them. God can handle His own defense."

I knew that my friend was right. Why had I felt the need to defend or explain God? Why couldn't I have been honest with the father and myself and say, "I don't know. But I do know that God loves us and God doesn't want us to hurt"?

Just like I did, Martha does what people of action do: She gives the "right" answer and prepares to move on. She gives the right answer, going so far as to affirm the orthodox Jewish belief in the life to come. And all the while, her real questions—her deep-in-the-soul questions—go unasked and thus unanswered.

Let me say this clearly: *God is not afraid of our expectations, doubts or questions.*

I know I have said it before, but why do I, and maybe you, need to hear it so often? Because as the disciples lacked courage and Thomas lacked hope, Martha's reaction reminds us what happens when we lack *honesty* when we confront our spiritual struggles.

Despite her equivocation, Jesus replies to Martha with firm and clear words of hope. He announces that *He* is the resurrection and the life. What crazy words, uttered in the middle of a mourning period, standing at the door of a tomb! But He says them, and He intends that we hear them. Christians die physical deaths, but Jesus is talking about *real* life, the kind not burdened by pain and loss and grief.

But Martha misses it. She is so busy trying to make sense of the situation *for* Jesus that she misses His words of comfort for that day and every day to come.

When Mary hears that Jesus has arrived, she, like Martha, goes immediately to meet Him—and so do all the mourners. The scene is freighted with drama. As Mary approaches Jesus, the group of wailing persons surrounds them. It's not only distressing, but it's annoying as well.

As Mary reaches Jesus, the scripture states that she kneels at Jesus' feet and cries, "If you had been here, my brother would not have died" (see John 11:32). She pours out her grief and confusion in a torrent of tears, unable to say anything else, and the scriptures state that Jesus, witnessing Mary's reaction, as well as the reaction of the mourners, is "deeply moved in spirit and troubled" (v. 33). *The New King James Version* says that He "groaned in the spirit." We need to catch this: The Messiah *groans in agony* at the grief He is witnessing.

Jesus' response, which we will examine more closely, tells us a great deal about the depth of Mary's grief. This situation is so far removed from the day when she had sat at Jesus' feet to learn about the kingdom of God! Now she kneels at His feet, wondering why her world has collapsed. As we explored earlier, Jesus loves this family and has great affection for Mary. Her deep emotional distress moves Him beyond words.

Mary is overwhelmed and confused. She had heard Jesus teach about life and hope, but how can she believe in such things now? She is wounded. Her faith has been tested and feels as though it is broken. Of the four reactions, Mary's is the saddest and most spiritually wrenching. Unlike the disciples, Thomas or even Martha, Mary's mouth utters a few words but her heart remains silent, too distraught to voice anything. If anyone can see this heart silence, it is Jesus.

Mary's pain is the deepest kind. She's not angry or frustrated, for those feelings are the opposite of peace and understanding—which is at least *something*. No, she is, as a theologian friend puts it, simply *without*. The groans from within Mary are the sounds of a soul for whom God has disappeared. It is her emptiness that draws Jesus' groans in response.

The disciples resisted. Thomas courageously followed. Martha gave the right answers. Mary simply gave up.

The four reactions explored above tell us much about the characters involved, but even more about ourselves. We see ourselves in these characters because death and mourning, of various kinds, are the great equalizers of humanity. Invariably, our true strengths and weaknesses emerge. Death knows no socioeconomic status, no nationality, no religion, no political persuasion, no good life or bad choices, no criminal or saint. The story of Lazarus is really the story of how we react when death and grief and trouble come a-knockin'; that is the reason for Jesus' tears.

Jesus didn't weep for Lazarus; he was in better shape than any of the others. Jesus wept for the mourners who were weeping without really knowing why. He wept for the disciples whose fears, once again, had gotten the best of them. He wept for Thomas, who had all the courage he needed but none of the hope he so desperately wanted. He wept for Martha, who could give the right answers but couldn't ask honest questions. And Jesus wept for Mary, who believed that God had vanished. But, friends, here is the beauty and burden of this passage: Jesus wept, too, for you and me, and for every lonely tomb before which we will ever stand.

That day at Lazarus' tomb, there were so many dead. Jesus stood in the midst of friends and strangers and followers and wondered why they couldn't see what He saw. *My disciples, you don't have to be afraid—I'm not. Thomas, you don't have to be a martyr—all you have to do is trust and follow and be amazed! Martha, don't you understand what I am saying? I'm not just fulfilling a religious objective—I'm talking about real life that lasts forever and makes this life look like a momentary displeasure. Mary . . . sweet Mary . . . don't give up— you sat at My feet for a reason. You knew that God was close that day. He is close now, even if you can't seem to find Him.*

Jesus stood there and looked from one to another, grieving all that death and wondering why it would continue to be so difficult for them and for us to see something better. Jesus wept for what they had done and had not done, for where they had been and for where they had refused to go. He wept for how the world had made them cynical, fearful, hopeless, confused and sad. The lump in His throat began to hurt and the hole in His heart began to throb, and it was too much . . .

He stood at the tomb, and the God of the universe wept. He wept because those He loved were living like they were already dead.

Jesus dries His tears and tells those who are gathered to move the stone from the entrance to Lazarus's tomb. Martha protests, "He would stink by now!" (see John 11:39). What could Jesus possibly want in removing the stone? Maybe to see Lazarus one more time? But by now, the fourth day, his face would be so disfigured that even Jesus would not recognize His friend. Yet with a touch of frustration, perhaps, Jesus replies, "Didn't I tell you, Martha, that you would see the glory of God?" (see John 11:40).
They roll the stone away, and Jesus steps forward to pray.

His prayer tells us much about God's cure for chronic death. He begins by making it plain to whom He is talking, wanting those around to see the connection between themselves, this event and the Father. Then He calls Lazarus forth. A few seconds pass . . . and then Lazarus appears! The moment should have been heralded by trumpets and great fanfare, but instead Jesus simply says, "Unwrap him and let him go" (see John 11:44). The scene is stark, simple yet powerful. It tells us how God works: He brings life where there was only death, and expects us to live like it.

In John 16:33, Jesus reminds His disciples, "In this world you will have trouble." I have often been struck by how true, but also how honest, a statement this is from God. In my life, I have known a lot of trouble. Hemophilia from birth, eye surgery, HIV and hepatitis-C, heart surgery—should I go on? I have also known the more personal, relational problems as well—broken friendships, betrayal, bad choices, the hurtful decisions of others. Yep, Jesus is right. In this world we have trouble. But if you think about it, it's pretty great of God to come out and admit it. He doesn't beat around the bush or paint flowery pictures— He's completely honest and straightforward: *Guys, while you are here, it may get pretty bad . . .*

And then He goes on: "But take heart, for I have overcome the world." Notice that Jesus doesn't say your troubles will get better or that your life will be easy. No, Jesus says to "take heart." I love that phrase. It comes from an ancient understanding of the relationship between parts of the body and different kinds of courage. Physical courage is found in the stomach, but the courage that causes someone to move through what seems to be a hopeless situation comes from the heart.

Through Jesus, God understands the troubles of this life and has made a way for us to "take heart" and begin to truly live. How did God do this? It goes something like this: God loved us and decided that we were worth dying for. God, in Jesus, came into the muck to become like us, not only to rectify the cosmic gulf between Him and us, but also to restore the brokenness in and between people. In doing so, God called us out of the tombs in which we sealed ourselves, unwrapped us from our doubt and sin and misery, and set us free.

But, friend, it is still up to us to come forth and be willing to be alive again. We have to stop living like those walking around dead, and start walking like a dead person who has been raised from the tomb. We must live like Lazarus.

Reflection Questions

John 11 runs deeper than the miracle it describes. The encounter begins with the confusion and misunderstanding of the disciples. Then Thomas speaks up with plenty of courage, but missing genuine hope. Next we find Martha lamenting to Jesus, "If you had only been here." She says the right words, but she doesn't share her honest feelings. Mary arrives wanting to believe, though the grief is too great even for words. And finally, of course, we have Lazarus, still in the tomb, the involuntary center of the drama. By the end, we see hearts and faiths struggling to understand Jesus' proclamation that life and death belong in God's hands. Jesus raises Lazarus and entreats some bystanders to free him from his burial cloths; after all, why should living folks live like dead ones? The four different reactions to Jesus and the situation leave us to wonder who the "dead ones" in the story really are.

The Bible says to "give our worries and cares to God because He cares for you" (1 Peter 5:7). God grieves to watch His children live as those who don't know the real source of life. Which character are you in the story? What keeps you from seeing God's hand working at the tombs of your life? In what ways do you need to be honest with God?

_____

_____

_____

_____

_____

Why does a crisis make us stop and cherish people, places and moments more? Think of those moments you wish you could revisit in your life. Why? What are some ways you can treasure what is most important to you before the crisis comes?

_____

_____

_____

_____

_____

To whom do you need to reconnect today? What has kept those relationships broken or strained?

_____

_____

_____

Heavenly Father, open up my heart and mind to Your Word so that I recognize what prophecies have been fulfilled and what is yet to come. Let my faith be strong like Noah and Abraham so that I will obey without questioning. Lord, please keep the spark of first love in my heart, words and actions. Amen.

Matthew 21:1-11 (NIV)

[1]As they approached Jerusalem and came to Bethphage on the Mount of Olives, Jesus sent two disciples, [2]saying to them, "Go to the village ahead of you, and at once you will find a donkey tied there, with her colt by her. Untie them and bring them to me. [3]If anyone says anything to you, say that the Lord needs them, and he will send them right away."

[4]This took place to fulfill what was spoken through the prophet:

[5]"Say to Daughter Zion,
   'See, your king comes to you,

   gentle and riding on a donkey,

   and on a colt, the foal of a donkey.'"

[6]The disciples went and did as Jesus had instructed them. [7]They brought the donkey and the colt and placed their cloaks on them for Jesus to sit on. [8]A very large crowd spread their cloaks on the road, while others cut branches from the trees and spread them on the road. [9]The crowds that went ahead of him and those that followed shouted,

   "Hosanna to the Son of David!"
   "Blessed is he who comes in the name of the Lord!"
   "Hosanna in the highest heaven!"

[10]When Jesus entered Jerusalem, the whole city was stirred and asked, "Who is this?"

[11]The crowds answered, "This is Jesus, the prophet from Nazareth in Galilee."

Devotion

Matthew 21:1-5

It is the beginning of the Passover, and Jesus was preparing to go to Jerusalem to celebrate. As He was getting ready to enter the city, Jesus sent two disciples to go into the gates of Jerusalem. There they will find a donkey tied to a post. They are to bring it back for Jesus to ride on as he enters the city. This is fulfilling the prophecy in Zechariah 9:9, which states, "Rejoice greatly, Daughter Zion! Shout, Daughter Jerusalem! See, your king comes to you, righteous and victorious, lowly and riding on a donkey, on a colt, the foal of a donkey." It is important to notice that Jesus did not enter proudly on a war horse but humbly on a donkey.

Matthew 21:6-7

The disciples went and did exactly as Jesus had instructed. No questions asked. They simply OBEYED. Nothing is recorded about the owner of the donkey. Could he have possibly known God's word? Did he know Zechariah 9:9? Did he willingly hand over the donkey? All we know is that the disciples took the donkey to Jesus. It appears that the animal's owner also OBEYED!

Matthew 21:8-9

As Jesus enters Jerusalem, the people line the streets, spreading their cloaks and branches on the road singing, "Hosanna to the Son of David." Again, prophecy is fulfilled. Just as Psalm 118:26 says, the people proclaim, "Blessed is he who comes in the name of the Lord. From the house of the Lord, we bless you."

Matthew 21:10-11

When asked, "Who is this?" the crowd recognized Jesus as the prophet from Nazareth. But within a few days, the same people would shout, "Crucify Him!"

These few verses reveal:

- PROPHECY fulfilled
- OBEDIENCE to Christ
- JOY in knowing and recognizing Christ

Reflection Questions

- Are you Bible literate enough to know and recognize fulfilled prophecy? What does Jesus' voluntarily humility tell us about how He saves us? Make a list of some of the prophecies Jesus fulfilled. Name some other prophecies yet to be fulfilled.

_____

_____

_____

_____

•Do you question your obedience to Christ, or are you eager to obey, even when it seems silly at the time? When was the last time you stepped out in faith and obeyed? Name some people who revealed their faith by their OBEDIENCE. Read Hebrews 11.

_____

_____

_____

_____

•How long after a retreat, good sermon or lecture has your zeal for Christ lasted? Did you make it past three days? What can you do to keep this love and jubilation at its peak?

_____

_____

_____

_____

Heavenly Father, I thank You for the time I have had with You this morning. I thank You every morning for listening to my concerns, for reassuring me that whatever trials I encounter I am never alone. I am thankful that You are with me to navigate my way through each of my challenges. Father, let me be ever mindful that I should turn to You first for my needs and not in desperation as a last resort. Forgive my shortcomings and my sins. Guide me this day, for it is in Your name that I pray. Amen.

Isaiah 50:4-9 (NIV)

> ⁴The Sovereign Lord has given me a well-instructed tongue,
>   to know the word that sustains the weary.
> He wakens me morning by morning,
>   wakens my ear to listen like one being instructed.
> ⁵The Sovereign Lord has opened my ears;
>   I have not been rebellious,
>   I have not turned away.
> ⁶I offered my back to those who beat me,
>   my cheeks to those who pulled out my beard;
> I did not hide my face
>   from mocking and spitting.
> ⁷Because the Sovereign Lord helps me,
>   I will not be disgraced.
> Therefore have I set my face like flint,
>   and I know I will not be put to shame.
> ⁸He who vindicates me is near.
>   Who then will bring charges against me?
>   Let us face each other!
> Who is my accuser?
>   Let him confront me!
> ⁹It is the Sovereign Lord who helps me.
>   Who will condemn me?
> They will all wear out like a garment;
>   the moths will eat them up.

Devotion

My eyes "blink" open. It is 6:00 in the morning and still dark outside. The house is so quiet. My wife and children are still asleep, and so is the dog. The sun has not risen, but God's Son has been awake. He's been with me all night eager to "awaken me morning by morning" and to hear my early greeting. Right now, at this very time, I can focus on Him. I can talk with Him and not be distracted. I can reach for His Word (the Bible), rather than my emails, cell phone or the sports page.

IT IS MY TIME TO BE WITH HIM! Some people call it QUIET TIME. Others call it CENTERING TIME, a moment to center our souls in Christ. Call it what you wish, but it is my daily time to fellowship with the Lord. QUIET TIME is a perfect time to pray for strength to face the challenges and opportunities of the day. Jesus often got alone with His Father, such as the time He prayed in the Garden of Gethsemane for strength to face and endure what was forthcoming. It has been said, "Sufferings in life are shared experiences with Jesus."

When we are troubled or concerned about a future event, take it to our Lord. When someone (Satan) or some group is attacking us personally or challenging our beliefs, take it to our Lord and trust in Him. Jesus did! Isaiah did! Why shouldn't we do the same? Jesus can hardly wait to speak a word, at just the right time, to one who is weary. He does this for our benefit so that we might pass His refreshing word on to others who are weary. Jesus told His disciples that He would always be with them, and He tells us the same even to the end of time.

Rev. Billy Graham has said, "The highest joy in my life has been my fellowship with Jesus." Celebrate fellowship with Jesus the first thing each morning. After all, He has been with us all night awaiting our awakening.

Reflection Questions

•During my quiet time, am I listening or always the one doing the talking? "Listen to my instruction and be wise. Don't ignore it." (Proverbs 8:33, NLT)

_____

_____

•When I am in trouble, how can I count on God to hear my prayers? "When you call on me, when you come and pray to me, I'll listen. When you come looking for me, you'll find me." (Jeremiah 29:12-13, MSG)

_____

_____

•When I feel I am walking alone, is God really walking beside me? "He will keep you strong to the end...for he is faithful to do what he says, and he has invited you into partnership with his Son, Jesus Christ our Lord." (I Corinthians 1:8-9, NLT).

_____

_____

Psalm 31:9-16 | Rebekah Kessler

Dear Jesus, Thank You for being my rock and the lifter of my head. When I feel that I am in the depths of despair, I know I can look to You and You will lift me up. Thank You for Your mercy and strength. Daily may I say, 'But I trust in You, O Lord,' I say, 'You are my God. My times are in Your hands.' Amen.

Psalm 31:9-16 (NIV)

⁹Be merciful to me, Lord, for I am in distress;

 my eyes grow weak with sorrow,

 my soul and body with grief.
¹⁰My life is consumed by anguish

 and my years by groaning;

 my strength fails because of my affliction,

 and my bones grow weak.
¹¹Because of all my enemies,

 I am the utter contempt of my neighbors

 and an object of dread to my closest friends—

 those who see me on the street flee from me.
¹²I am forgotten as though I were dead;

 I have become like broken pottery.
¹³For I hear many whispering,

 "Terror on every side!"

 They conspire against me

 and plot to take my life.

¹⁴But I trust in you, Lord;

 I say, "You are my God."
¹⁵My times are in your hands;

 deliver me from the hands of my enemies,

from those who pursue me.
¹⁶Let your face shine on your servant;
   save me in your unfailing love.

Devotion

My mind goes back to six years ago when I was in deep sorrow and mourning. I had no enemies trailing after me or people trying to kill me, but there was a definite battle going on for my soul. My mother, who was my rock, my compass and my best friend, was diagnosed with pancreatic cancer in October 2007. She passed away three months later. I stayed with my mom a lot and experienced every emotion imaginable. There were times when I would question God, times I would get angry and even times I would laugh because of something my mother had done. Some of the times when a family member would come to relieve me, I would go home, lay on my bed and just cry. This was a very hard time for my family and me. We knew and believed God could heal her but believed in His sovereignty if he chose not to.

When she did pass away, the spiritual and emotional fog started to roll in. This is the time when I completely related to the distress David describes in this passage. I was so weak and weary from the loss and the aftermath that followed.

How could the God of love and mercy we all believed in possibly let this happen? My mother had done so much in her ministry to others as a hairdresser for 40 plus years. She had helped chemotherapy patients, rescued women from abusive relationships and done so much for single moms. She was our family's spiritual rock and the glue that held everything together.

For months after her death, I would have dreams that seemed so real that she was alive and just had been on a long vacation. We would sit and drink coffee and laugh about all kinds of things. I would tell her how much her granddaughter had grown and all the funny things she was doing. I would ask all the wife and mother questions I had wanted to but never found the time. I was exhausted, and there was nothing other than God's grace through faithful friends and family that drew me out of this pit of despair. My husband was an amazing source of strength throughout the process and still is to this day.

The fog started to clear as I spent more time in the word and prayer. In verse 14 David says "But I trust in you, Lord; I say, 'You are my God.'" This was life to me, I was able to realize that God had everything covered, and He was in control. Yes, to this day I am heartbroken that my mom is not here to see her grandkids grow and give me wise counsel, but I also am confident that I will see her again one day.

Reflection Questions

•Have you ever felt a time of distress and despair?

_____

_____

•In times of anguish and weakness, what can you do to get out of the pit?

_____

_____

_____

_____

•Take time and reflect on a time of joy and blessing. How would this memory help in a time of despair?

_____

_____

_____

_____

_____

_____

_____

God Almighty, we pray that You open our eyes and our hearts to the depth of the humility that You have demonstrated for us in the sacrifice that was made in Christ Jesus. Help us to gain a better comprehension of what it truly means to be imitators of Christ. May we gain a better understanding of how every facet of Your character teaches us the ultimate goal of life, to bring glory and honor to Your name. Amen.

Philippians 2:5-11 (ESV)

> [5]Have this mind among yourselves, which is yours in Christ Jesus, [6]who, though he was in the form of God, did not count equality with God a thing to be grasped, [7]but emptied himself, by taking the form of a servant, being born in the likeness of men. [8]And being found in human form, he humbled himself by becoming obedient to the point of death, even death on a cross. [9]Therefore God has highly exalted him and bestowed on him the name that is above every name, [10]so that at the name of Jesus every knee should bow, in heaven and on earth and under the earth, [11]and every tongue confess that Jesus Christ is Lord, to the glory of God the Father.

Devotion

We live in a culture that likes mathematics. We don't understand grace very well, even though we proudly proclaim that we no longer have to live under the Law. We don't understand grace because we can't keep track of it mathematically. In a culture of law, when we break a rule, we pay a fine. We keep track of our debts, and then we pay off each one. It's simple math. You invite me to dinner, and I invite you to dinner. If I fail to invite you, then I become the less charitable friend. Our mistakes, our relationships and our choices are all guided by our calculations.

Grace doesn't fit into our logical, quantitative world. But without grace, we could have no salvation. We could never reconcile all of the debts that we have created against God. The Father knows that in order to bring grace into our world, He will have to completely revolutionize the relationship. In the Incarnation, He not only paves the way for salvation, but also the way for imitation.

When Christ is on the cross, He is not simply rescuing us. He is also setting an example for us in obedience, humility and worship. God wants so much more than simply providing us with a pardon. He wants to see His creation restored to its original intent. He wants us to learn to glorify Him through character and obedience. What better way to demonstrate this to us than through the cross!

Reflection Questions

•How is God's economy and culture different from ours?

_____

_____

_____

_____

•How does my life look like Christ's?

_____

_____

_____

_____

•How does obedience help build humility?

_____

_____

_____

_____

_____

Father, teach me to believe in Your benevolence before I can see it. Help me to follow with my heart, not my head. Lord, help me to realize that trusting usually does not involve understanding. Amen.

Matthew 27:11-54 (NIV)

[11]Meanwhile Jesus stood before the governor, and the governor asked him, "Are you the king of the Jews?"

"You have said so," Jesus replied.

[12]When he was accused by the chief priests and the elders, he gave no answer. [13]Then Pilate asked him, "Don't you hear the testimony they are bringing against you?" [14]But Jesus made no reply, not even to a single charge—to the great amazement of the governor.

[15]Now it was the governor's custom at the festival to release a prisoner chosen by the crowd. [16]At that time they had a well-known prisoner whose name was Jesus Barabbas. [17]So when the crowd had gathered, Pilate asked them, "Which one do you want me to release to you: Jesus Barabbas, or Jesus who is called the Messiah?" [18]For he knew it was out of self-interest that they had handed Jesus over to him.

[19]While Pilate was sitting on the judge's seat, his wife sent him this message: "Don't have anything to do with that innocent man, for I have suffered a great deal today in a dream because of him."

[20]But the chief priests and the elders persuaded the crowd to ask for Barabbas and to have Jesus executed.

[21]"Which of the two do you want me to release to you?" asked the governor.

"Barabbas," they answered.

[22]"What shall I do, then, with Jesus who is called the Messiah?" Pilate asked.

They all answered, "Crucify him!"

[23]"Why? What crime has he committed?" asked Pilate.

But they shouted all the louder, "Crucify him!"

[24]When Pilate saw that he was getting nowhere, but that instead an uproar was starting, he took water and washed his hands in front of the crowd. "I am innocent of this man's blood," he said. "It is your responsibility!"

[25]All the people answered, "His blood is on us and on our children!"

[26]Then he released Barabbas to them. But he had Jesus flogged, and handed him over to be crucified.

[27]Then the governor's soldiers took Jesus into the Praetorium and gathered the whole company of soldiers around him. [28]They stripped him and put a scarlet robe on him, [29]and then twisted together a crown of thorns and set it on his head. They put a staff in his right hand. Then

they knelt in front of him and mocked him. "Hail, king of the Jews!" they said. [30]They spit on him, and took the staff and struck him on the head again and again. [31]After they had mocked him, they took off the robe and put his own clothes on him. Then they led him away to crucify him. [32]As they were going out, they met a man from Cyrene, named Simon, and they forced him to carry the cross. [33]They came to a place called Golgotha (which means "the place of the skull"). [34]There they offered Jesus wine to drink, mixed with gall; but after tasting it, he refused to drink it. [35]When they had crucified him, they divided up his clothes by casting lots. [36]And sitting down, they kept watch over him there. [37]Above his head they placed the written charge against him: this is jesus, the king of the jews.

[38]Two rebels were crucified with him, one on his right and one on his left. [39]Those who passed by hurled insults at him, shaking their heads [40]and saying, "You who are going to destroy the temple and build it in three days, save yourself! Come down from the cross, if you are the Son of God!" [41]In the same way the chief priests, the teachers of the law and the elders mocked him. [42]"He saved others," they said, "but he can't save himself! He's the king of Israel! Let him come down now from the cross, and we will believe in him. [43]He trusts in God. Let God rescue him now if he wants him, for he said, 'I am the Son of God.'" [44]In the same way the rebels who were crucified with him also heaped insults on him.

[45]From noon until three in the afternoon darkness came over all the land. [46]About three in the afternoon Jesus cried out in a loud voice, *"Eli, Eli, lema sabachthani?"* (which means "My God, my God, why have you forsaken me?").

[47]When some of those standing there heard this, they said, "He's calling Elijah."

[48]Immediately one of them ran and got a sponge. He filled it with wine vinegar, put it on a staff, and offered it to Jesus to drink. [49]The rest said, "Now leave him alone. Let's see if Elijah comes to save him."

[50]And when Jesus had cried out again in a loud voice, he gave up his spirit.

[51]At that moment the curtain of the temple was torn in two from top to bottom. The earth shook, the rocks split [52]and the tombs broke open. The bodies of many holy people who had died were raised to life. [53]They came out of the tombs after Jesus' resurrection and went into the holy city and appeared to many people.

[54]When the centurion and those with him who were guarding Jesus saw the earthquake and all that had happened, they were terrified, and exclaimed, "Surely he was the Son of God!"

Devotion

It is a question that has been asked since the beginning. How can God allow such awful things to happen to good people? We make allowances for judgment to fall on the evil-doer. We even have a name for it. We call it poetic justice. Well he got what he deserved. When the good, the young and the innocent are assaulted with sickness or personal disaster, we also have a word for that. t is called unfair!

In consideration of our text, there is a story, which to the disciples must have seemed like incontrovertible evidence that God is not in control of this world all the time. If He is in control, how can He be a benevolent God? No one asks these questions out loud. In moments of doubt and weakness, we ask them of ourselves. We dare not articulate our true feelings. What would people think?

Part of our moral DNA possesses a sense of fair play. This sense of fair play is found in the believer as well as the unbeliever. In Matthew 27:22, Pilate asked of the people, "What shall I do then with Jesus which is called Christ? They all say unto him, Let him be crucified." In verse 23, you see that sense of fairness being breeched when Pilate asks of the mob, "What evil hath he done?" (KJV) Even as an unbeliever, Pilate had a moral sense that this just wasn't fair. Pilate had a feeling in his "moral compass" there would be an accounting of this awful violation of innocence and fairness.

For Christians, we have the rest of the story. We know why Christ was promised in the Old Testament. We know why God became man in flesh. We know why He was unfairly accused, tortured and killed. Our redemption depended on this supreme act of sacrifice.

It is very interesting that in the last words of Jesus, He asked in Matthew 27:46 "My God, my God, why hast thou forsaken me?" (KJV) I do not believe Jesus was asking a rhetorical question. His question was real. Is there another way? Why are you so far away, My Father? I need You right now during this time of suffering.

With Christ as our example, when understanding stops, we must exercise our faith in God. We will never have all of the information we need to understand sickness, death of the young and personal disaster in our lives. We must believe that God is in control of this world and that He is benevolent.

Reflection Questions

•Have you ever questioned the goodness or fairness of God?

_____

_____

_____

_____

_____

_____

•Where does our sense of "fair play" originate? Are we born with it, or is it taught by our culture?

_____

_____

_____

_____

•Do you think the question of Christ in Matthew 27:46 in any way conveys the message that He thought God would be there with Him at the cross?

_____

_____

_____

_____

SUNDAY

SHANE STANFORD

JOHN 21:1-23, JOHN 18:15-27

Roman guards stationed in the city of Jerusalem divided the night into four *watches*, and at the end of the 3 A.M. to 6 A.M. watch, a trumpet sounded to indicate a change in the guard. The word describing this change, both from the Latin and Greek, means *cockcrow*. Which brings us to the human drama that unfolded between Jesus and Peter.

While sitting around the table for the Passover Meal, Jesus predicted that Peter would deny Him three times before the cockcrow. Peter was adamant that such a thing could not happen. Jesus simply looked at His friend, knowing the strength of words but weakness of action among His followers.

Of course, Peter was stronger than most. Reactionary, sure, but Peter never feared a challenge. He had been the only disciple to attempt to walk on the water (see Matthew 14:22-36), and lest we forget, while the other disciples were silent, Peter confessed Jesus as the Messiah (see Matthew 16:13-20). And yet, not too many steps into the sea, Peter began to sink, and not long after his glorious confession, Peter was rebuked by Jesus for misunderstanding His real mission.

Peter was brash, passionate and bold. And, although he had stumbled before, sitting around this table, he confidently proclaimed his unwavering support. Later, when the soldiers arrived with Judas to arrest Jesus, Peter grabbed a sword and defended his friend. Jesus stopped Peter's attack, but Peter had proven his point: He was a friend to the last.

Peter, maybe more than anyone else, represents the fragile nature of humanity, especially when the world becomes too real. After Jesus is arrested and taken to the high priest's home, the mounting anxiety takes hold. The other disciples flee, and though Peter follows Jesus, he lags far behind. He moves from shadow to shadow, staying close . . . but not *too* close.

Another disciple lets Peter into the courtyard of the high priest's palace. Here, Peter hears the discussion and wants more than anything to defend his friend. But for some reason, he is not as brave now. Time and the night have drained his courage, and he stands silent.

A maid is the first to recognize him. "Aren't you a follower of Jesus?" she asks. "I am not," Peter replies (see John 18:17). He moves quickly away.

A second time, a group of servants recognize Peter and ask if he is a follower of Jesus. Again, he denies it (see John 18:25).

Finally, another person asks, "Aren't you one of Jesus' followers?" Peter turns and, with a curse, denies his friend a third time (see John 18:26-27).

Just then, the trumpet for the guard change sounds the cockcrow. It is over. Jesus was right.

It's ironic. As Jesus is taken away, bound and beaten, accused of confessing that He is "I AM," Peter becomes all of us, hiding behind our fear, crying, "I am not."

Does Peter's behavior surprise you, or are you so familiar with this story that you've forgotten how to be shocked by such a stunning betrayal? Or perhaps Peter's treachery feels personal because you have had a Peter in your life who has betrayed you. I have.

Now, keep in mind that my life is an open book. Since the day I stood before a small church in southern Mississippi and asked them why they didn't want me to be their pastor, only to hear them respond, "Because you have HIV," I have allowed people into my life and thoughts. I have written about most of my interactions and feelings as an HIV-positive minister, sharing what it has been like to deal with the uncertainties such a condition creates. I have shared my journey before thousands of people. For years I have told my story, sometimes at the consternation of others, sometimes at their request, but I rarely hold anything back.

But I don't talk about betrayal much. As open as my life is in one sense, betrayal is just too personal in another.

The betrayal happened without my knowledge. Sure, I suspected that my friendship with this person possessed broken edges, and people had warned me about unhealthy patterns they had seen, but I tend to give people the benefit of the doubt. As it turned out, this worked against me.

The cock crowed on a Monday morning. The news of my betrayal was first revealed, and it was bad. The level of deception and duplicity went beyond anything I could have imagined. The details flowed in, running like venom mixed with tears. With one truth came another lie that led to more questions, followed by more confessions that pointed to more lies. Before it was over, the meaning of an entire five-year period of my life had been reduced to rubble. The friend, who, to his credit, had stopped the destructive patterns some time before the confession, had created a façade to protect his self-interests, and when the truth finally emerged, it became clear that no one else could know about it. The repercussions would have been too great. Leaked details would have affected not only my friend and me, but also our families and children. It was like a bomb had exploded, without anyone knowing the carnage it had caused.

Even with the shock and pain, I never thought of doing anything drastic, such as suicide or violence, though for the first time in my life, I could understand how someone might see such actions as solutions. I discovered that, when one has been betrayed, there is a need to do something, to find a way to make the pain stop. Oh, did I mention the pain? Even after growing up a hemophiliac with bleeding muscles and joints and taking medicines that make me feel horrible, I have never felt anything more painful than betrayal. There is no running from it, no sedation for it, no cure. It just hurts.

And then there was the rage. I am not an angry person by nature, but with betrayal, "by nature" is thrown out the window. We become, no matter who we are, "reactors," dangerously churning powerful, barely contained emotions on the inside.

Betrayal also brought self-doubt. *Where did I go wrong? What could I have done differently? Why did I trust him? What is wrong with me?* These were only the first questions. Before long, self-doubt became humiliation partnered with paranoia. *What if others find out? What if people knew what has happened? Would they be laughing at me? What about my family? What would they think?* Question after question, with scarcely a pause between them.

And then betrayal brought the worst of its plagues: hopelessness. *If he did this to me, what makes me think others aren't doing it or won't do it, too?* Before long, betrayal affects every corner of your life, including your spiritual core. After all, the roots of betrayal began there.

Betrayal was born at the beginning, in the Garden of Eden, and it has infected us ever since. Picture it: Adam and Eve are having a grand time. They have their jobs (taking care of creation) and each other and, most importantly, they have God. I love the scripture passage that says God was "walking in the garden in the cool of the day" (Genesis 3:8). What a scene! The Creator takes a stroll, looking for the pride of His creation. The feel of the passage is that God has walked here before with Adam and Eve and that He enjoys this time with them. Adam and Even don't see creation as work or a struggle; they experience God at His most personal, living as friends do. Things are perfect. The world is right.

But all too soon, the serpent spoke a beautiful, well-crafted lie, and Adam and Eve toyed with being their own gods. Oddly enough, I don't think they ever meant to hurt God. Most betrayals are not premeditated, but they are personal—and this was the first and most personal of all. Betrayal killed what held creation together. It was relational murder on a cosmic scale.

Adam and Eve, for the most basic and selfish of reasons, killed their relationship with God. They chose momentary pleasure—the thought of becoming their own rulers—over the long-term joy of knowing and walking in the cool of the day with the Creator. After the first bite of betrayal, Adam and Eve had only to look at themselves, ashamed by their nakedness for the first time, to realize what they had done. *What just happened here? You made me do it! No, it was your idea!* And then Adam and Eve did what murderers do. They fled, hid and crafted their alibis, even though they knew there were none.

With this, the effects of the most grievous of betrayals took hold in all of us. What seemed impossible perfection became imperfect. Adam and Eve not only turned on God, they turned on each other. Their souls became infected with the lie of self-sufficiency, and they had no alternative but to believe it—and to make more lies and, thus, more mistakes.

The scene shifts in Genesis 3:9-12 when God calls out, "Where are you?"

Adam responds, "I heard you but I was afraid because I was naked."

"Who told you that you were naked?" God asks.

"The woman *You* put here with me—she gave me some fruit from the tree, and I ate it."

Then God says to the woman, "What is this you have done?"

"The *serpent* deceived me, and I ate," she says, in a classic example of the blame game. Gone not only was the notion of relationship, but also the truth and any sense of personal responsibility. But as bad as it was, that was not the worst of it. There was more to come.

The passage says that Adam named Eve *after* the betrayal. Before, they had not needed names because they really knew one another. Betrayal broke not only the nature of relationship; it dissolved its possibilities. Gone was the potential of one person living in real fellowship with another and enjoying the blessing of the Creator. Now they hid behind their garments and names, always aware that something stood between everyone—people and people, and people and God.

For you see, that was the worst damage of this first betrayal, not that it broke these relationships (which was pretty damaging), but that it created in all of us a primal urge toward self-preservation. After all, when betrayal enters the picture, who can you trust?

But God knew exactly what would happen. That's why He tried to steer Adam and Eve away from choosing betrayal: "Don't eat of this tree. Don't take this first step, because once you do there is no going back. There is nothing on the other side of this fence but heartache and malice and rage and pain. I'm warning you, not because I am keeping something 'good' from you, but because I am protecting you. You can't handle this. You can't rationalize this. You can't manage this. *This will kill you*" (see Genesis 2:16-17).

It's been killing us ever since—killing us with vengeance when we are betrayed, and killing us with shame at our own treachery. And, friend, until a cross appeared on a hill and a stone was rolled away, that was the end of the story.

As the cockcrow sounds, Peter leaves the courtyard humiliated, dejected, angry, frustrated and ashamed. He leaves too human for his own skin, slipping away under the cover of darkness, much like Adam and Eve leaving the Garden. While his act of betrayal was unthinkable and his escape humiliating, it's the unbearable shame that hurts most.

This is our disease: We are afflicted by a lie that we too easily believe. As long as humans walk this earth—from Adam and Eve to Peter, from Peter to us—the cycle plays out: the *real* human drama in the *real* world, where people die from their secrets one guilty, painful, shameful breath at a time.

I believe that Peter went to the high priest's courtyard the night of Jesus' betrayal with other intentions, too. I believe he went there for his friend and that he had every intention of helping Jesus. You don't go from cutting off a person's ear in defense of your friend to denying that same friend in one large leap.

No, Peter is caught off guard—he's not prepared to find himself standing at the door of the enemy's house having to make a decision, at first about his friend but ultimately about himself. What if he thinks for just a second that he can get away with the first lie, or that maybe he can even control it? Then he might be able to help Jesus! And so, the first denial happens almost haphazardly. It isn't premeditated or even personal. The first steps in betrayal usually aren't. After all, the serpent didn't need to begin his conversation with Eve by asking if she would like to screw up all of humanity. No, he simply hissed, "Did God really say you couldn't eat of any fruit in the Garden?" (see Genesis 3:1). And the game was on.

Later, Peter stands around the campfire, feeling guilty for what he has just done, but still determined to help his friend, when he's asked the second time about his relationship with Jesus. He panics this time, and without much warning, he denies Jesus again. *Oh, no,* he thinks. *What am I doing?* Peter is no longer in control and the momentum is against him. He staggers from the gathering, only to be confronted again. The Adversary doesn't even need to lie to him any longer; Peter now believes the situation is hopeless. The Enemy only needs to place one more obstacle in Peter's path: Another servant appears, asking the same question of Peter, implying that he knows Jesus. One more denial, and just like that, the crock crows. It is finished.

What just happened here? Peter wonders as he flees from the high priest's home in shame. *I came here for better reasons. This isn't supposed to be how it turned out! How did it come to this?* I'll tell you: one little flinch of the soul at a time, until Jesus' boldest disciple ran like a coward from the scene, convinced that he had gone too far to ever call Jesus "Friend" again.

Yet because of a place called Calvary, this was not the end of Peter's story—and it's not the end of ours, either. But why is the new chapter so difficult to write? Because, like it our not, the previous chapters of our lives mean something and have an effect on us. They are not neat and easy. We can't help but replay the past and relive the mistakes. No matter how we read them, we can't walk away from the last chapters of our lives without understanding how ingrained the illness of the Adversary is in us.

It causes us to lie, cheat, hurt, deny and betray. It infects us at the most basic level, and once the disease grows, we lose our way, forget where we came from and end up living far, far away from our real home. As long as the Adversary can separate us from God and from each other, he can muddy the waters of God's grace enough that we are not sure if God can work in the midst of someone like us, even if there is a place called Calvary with a cross, and an empty tomb with the stone rolled away.

If we fail to acknowledge how deeply the previous chapters of our lives have scarred us, our "gospel" is too cheap. It is a gospel that does not understand the incredible magnitude of what Jesus did and does in and for us. He didn't just rectify a spiritual condition or pay a debt—no, He charged into the middle of a calamity that sought nothing less than to kill us.

So it is that Peter's Jesus-encounter sheds light on the rest of the encounters we have visited in this book. We feel utterly isolated, separated from God and others, because of too much—too much sin, too many mistakes, too much confusion, too much doubt, too much death—and we cheat our brothers and sisters (Zacchaeus), sell our bodies (woman caught in adultery), fear for our children's futures (man with the sick child), hate ourselves so that we despise everyone else (woman at the well), collapse under the burden of grief (Lazarus and friends), and yes, betray our best friends for no better reason than that we are afraid.

We're accustomed to lions eating zebras in this world because it's all that we have ever known.

Because we are so accustomed to this lions-eating-zebras world, the crucifixion of Jesus doesn't disturb us the way that it should. Most Christians envision a sanitized version of the Crucifixion— they have forgotten how truly gruesome it is. The one being crucified literally suffocates to death from the weight of his organs tearing in two. Finally, mercifully, the legs are broken and death is imminent. For those watching, the scene is unbearable. There is no honor in crucifixion. It is a criminal's death, a barbaric act reserved for the most reviled in society.

Thus, it must have been difficult to watch a man like Jesus be crucified, especially for those who loved Him most. They knew Him, and they knew His love for others. They had watched His compassionate ways and witnessed His miracles. He was no criminal. But what could they do? The Romans were in charge—the authorities had decreed a death sentence. So Jesus was hung and died. By the end, only the women who loved Him remained. The men fled or watched from a distance. Crucifixion is not just about death; it is abandonment at the most personal level.

I can only imagine Peter's thoughts as he watched his friend die. I don't know if Peter remained on the scene or not. There is no record of his presence at the cross, but I can't help but think that he stayed—at a distance, sure, but close enough to watch. Maybe it is my fanciful opinion or my need to give everyone the benefit of the doubt, but I just can't believe that Peter, even after the denial, would have left his friend.

Of course, Peter knew things would never be the same. Jesus would die alone. Peter couldn't help Him, and he didn't have the courage to die with Him. Yet Peter's failure was in being too human, not in faking his love for Jesus. He wasn't brave anymore. He wasn't brash. But he also wasn't pretending when he professed his love for his friend. I believe Peter would have found a way to the scene.

He would have watched the moans and seen the agony. He would have seen the final breath. He would have witnessed Jesus' body being taken down, and he would have watched as they placed Him in a borrowed tomb. And I believe Peter would have turned away after the stone was rolled in place, wondering what would become of what was left of his soul.

The time following the Crucifixion was difficult. We often forget that before the glory of Sunday morning, Saturday dragged on in a nothingness that seemed as if it would never end. It wasn't the pain and agony of Friday. It was worse; it was *nothing*, like most "next days" are after a disaster.

Then on Sunday, Mary Magdalene announces that she had seen Jesus, and Peter and John race to the tomb. Scripture says that John outruns Peter. I've wondered if John really outruns him or if Peter hangs back, afraid of what he might find. I'm sure he has mixed emotions. No one wants Jesus to be alive more than Peter. But what if Jesus is alive? Certainly, He couldn't have forgotten what had happened at the high priest's house. The questions race in Peter's mind, punctuated with one phrase: *Jesus died alone.* Peter—first out of the boat, first to confess Jesus as Messiah—can never forgive himself for that. And he can't imagine that Jesus could, either. The horror of the Crucifixion was unspeakable, but the nails Peter drives into his own conscience are terrible, too.

To his amazement, Peter finds the tomb empty, and he re- turns to tell the disciples the news. Jesus appears to the disciples several times in the following days. Each time is magnificent, but even glory has limits when it comes to the human heart. With Jesus' resurrection, the real issue for Peter has little to do with stones rolled way or mystical appearances behind locked doors. No, one question remains: *Can one friend forgive another for doing the unforgivable?*

As is the case with most of us when tough times consume our lives, Peter returns to what he knows; he goes fishing. This may seem odd in the middle of the Resurrection appearances, but for a fisherman who believes his relationship with Jesus is perma- nently changed (even in light of the Resurrection miracle), where else would Peter go? Several of the disciples join him. The disciples fish without much success. That changes when a figure calls out from the shore, "Have you caught any fish?"

"No," they reply.

"Then cast your nets on the right side of the boat," the figure says (see John 21:6). As- suming it couldn't hurt, the disciples do what the man says.

The scripture says that the catch is so great that the disciples can't haul the net into their boat. In fact, they drag the net full of fish to shore. But this story isn't about fishing. As the nets fill with fish, Peter's heart fills with something else—the familiar voice of One who he once knew well. John is the first to recognize Jesus: "It is the Lord!" he says (see John 21:7). Peter gets dressed, jumps from the boat and swims ashore.

Now this passage contains some important events that should not be missed, including the number of fish in the catch, why Peter was fishing naked and why the "right side" of the boat was significant. In truth, this is one of the most important passages for the Early Church, especially in relation to the mission of the first followers. (I discuss this passage in depth in my book *The Seven Next Words of Christ*.)

But the heart of the story is Peter and Jesus. When Peter recognizes Jesus on the shore, he sees more than a familiar face. This is Peter's chance for redemption. Locked rooms, empty tombs and the previous encounters with Jesus after His Resurrection meant wonderful things about the majesty of God's power, but they didn't answer the questions in Peter's heart.

This scene is different; it is personal. Peter had heard Jesus call from the shoreline before. This is *their* scene. In Luke 5, Jesus called the first disciples, Peter among them, while they were fishing. "Put out into deep water, and let down the nets for a catch," Jesus said (v. 4), and the rest was history. Today's calling, so reminiscent of that first day, is about redemption and restoration, and Peter knows it from the moment John calls out Jesus' name. Peter swims ashore and joins Jesus around the campfire—he knows his moment has arrived.

Jesus turns to Peter and asks, "Simon, son of John, do you truly love me more than these?" (see John 21:15). Scholars have debated what "these" are. Maybe He is referring to the other disciples, but I suspect He is pointing to the sea, the boats and the life of a fisherman. Peter had returned to what he knew best. We all do. But Jesus has other things, more wonderful things, in store for him. As much as Peter loves fishing, Jesus needs Peter to love Him more.

Peter answers, "Yes, Lord, You know I love You."

Jesus replies, "Then feed My lambs" (see John 21:15).

It may seem odd that Jesus would ask a fisherman to become a shepherd, but this is a new life and a new start for Peter.

Jesus asks the question two more times, and Peter answers yes to both. The third time, the scripture says that Peter is grieved by Jesus' question, or at least by how many times He has asked. How many times had Peter denied Jesus? Right . . . three. This is more than an inquisition—the questions represent a reunion. The number three symbolizes completeness, but completeness often comes with discomfort and a price.

Peter's threefold denial had seemed an insurmountable and complete dissolution of his relationship with God. But a three-fold declaration of love gives Peter the chance to answer again, and this time he is ready. Peter's denials had been about holding on to old patterns and answers; his answers now are the chance to do it over and get it right this time.

Jesus meets Peter on the shore of the sea and on the shoreline of Peter's life, and He restores him in a way that Peter will recognize forever. Jesus uses more than words; He uses the art of moving on and beginning again. In giving Peter the task of loving the sheep, Peter will always remember Jesus' love for him.

The first time Jesus had called Peter from the sea, Peter followed into the unknown. This time, Peter follows as one completely known and completely restored.

Peter went on to do more than make things right. He fed the sheep and loved the lambs. To his end, Peter confessed that not only did he know Jesus, he also loved Him and would die for Him. According to ancient sources, Peter bravely preached the Good News of Jesus from Jerusalem to Antioch to Rome. Eventually, near the end of Nero's reign, Peter—the one who once denied Jesus and then watched Him die on a cross—was crucified himself, except that he asked to be hung upside down out of respect for his friend. No one questioned Peter's loyalty or his courage ever again.

Reflection Questions

Calling from the shoreline, Jesus invited the disciples, who were fishing, to have breakfast. Peter jumped from the boat and swam ashore. The chapter describes Jesus and the disciples sitting around the campfire as Jesus began to question Peter's love for Him.

The scene not only marks Peter's redemption; it unveils the key to his restoration: Christ knew Peter's future, and He wanted Peter to understand it as well. Just days before, Peter's ministry, not to mention his life, was in shambles, but Jesus not only forgave Peter, He offered him a chance to change the world—not with swords or rebellion, but through love and service. No one's past or present prevents God's love calling them into their future.

The Bible says that through Christ, God has brought us back to Him as friends (see Colossians 1:22). When the going gets rough, human nature returns us to those things we know best. Thus, the disciples went fishing, so Jesus met them on the shore. Where are the shorelines of your life from which Jesus calls for you, His friend, to return home?

_____

_____

_____

_____

_____

_____

The animated movie *Madagascar* suggests that lions eat zebras because that is all they have ever known. Why is the lie of self-sufficiency, told by Satan from the beginning, so easy to believe?

_____

_____

_____

Think about the nature of betrayal in your life. Why does betrayal hurt so much? Are there those who have betrayed you? Have you betrayed someone? Describe your emotions and what has prevented you from reconciling.

_____

_____

_____

_____

The Bible says that "since God loved us that much, we surely ought to love each other" (1 John 4:11). We are to love and forgive one another. Make a list of those whom you need to forgive. Make a list of those from whom you need forgiveness. What keeps you from taking the next steps toward reconciliation?

_____

_____

_____

26996733R00094

Made in the USA
Charleston, SC
24 February 2014